ALONE
AND
SURVIVING
by Rae Lindsay

WALKER AND COMPANY
NEW YORK

First published in the United States of America in 1977 by the Walker Publishing Company, Inc.

Published simultaneously in Canada by Fitzhenry & Whiteside, Limited, Toronto

ISBN: 0-8027-0557-X

Library of Congress Catalog Card Number: 76-39594

Printed in the United States of America

Book design by Robert Barto

10   9   8   7   6   5   4   3   2   1

To Mom and Dad, who are always there when I need them; to Maria, Sandy, and Rob, who need me as much as I need them; and to Alex, who needed me, and loved me, and whom I need and love still.

Contents

Acknowledgments

MY SPECIAL GRATITUDE GOES TO NINETY-THREE WIDOWS WHO SHARED THEIR DEEPEST THOUGHTS WITH ME TO SHARE, IN TURN, WITH TWELVE MILLION OTHERS.

I AM ALSO GREATLY APPRECIATIVE TO TWO VERY BENEVOLENT INSTITUTIONS WHOSE GRANTS MADE IT POSSIBLE FOR ME TO RESEARCH THIS BOOK: THE NEW JERSEY STATE COUNCIL ON THE ARTS, AND THE CENTER FOR RESEARCH ON WOMEN IN HIGHER EDUCATION AND THE PROFESSIONS (COSPONSORED BY THE FEDERATION OF ORGANIZATIONS FOR PROFESSIONAL WOMEN AND WELLESLEY COLLEGE).

ALONE
AND
SURVIVING

Introduction

There are perhaps half a dozen milestones in adult life that most women look forward to: marriage, the birth of the first baby, the first house, the tenth or twentieth wedding anniversary, the first grandchild. But there is one milestone few people talk or think about until after it happens to three out of four married women: they become widows.

Much attention is paid in our country to the plight of the nine million men and women who are unemployed, and rightly so, but few realize that an even greater number of Americans—twelve million widows and one million widowers—must also live through an upside-down period brought on by fate, not choice. The situation of American widows is very different from that of the millions who are divorced. Widows are a solid, but silent, mi-

1

nority with few champions. As one researcher put it, "Widows are not organized as a group. They have no political or economic clout."

Still, it's easy to toss the problem off as one that concerns those people who have already lived most of their lives and therefore have lovely memories to look back on and live on. Most of us are inclined to think of the stereotyped grayhaired widowed grandmother who holds more or less the same rank as the "spinster aunt."

The statistics blast this kind of thinking. The median age for "new" widows is 52; almost six million widows are middle-aged or younger; further, one out of four widows is under 45. More mind-boggling is the fact that one out of six women over 21 is a widow. You can talk and think about merry widows, too, but in reality, the average widow lives on little more than $6,000 a year—which doesn't make for too much merriment. Remember, this figure is based on the widows who have inherited rather large insurance and property bequests as well as the millions subsisting on minimal incomes.

In this book I emphasize the problems of widows from 35 to 55, who often are not only faced with incredible financial problems, but must also cope with the day-to-day dilemma of bringing up children, paying off the mortgage, meeting the professional challenges of finding a fulfilling job (when all too often, they have been housewives for too many years), and the abrupt and traumatic business of getting back into the "singles scene."

The widow has been assigned a leper's role in society, because quite simply, nobody wants to be a widow, including Jacqueline Kennedy Onassis. Even the active women's liberation groups, such as N.O.W., turn away from the problems of widows. I am not suggesting a militant conspiracy to change this attitude, and I offer no simplistic program for organizing widows. Rather, having been widowed at a more or less tender age with three children under 11, I've found not only a need to compare my feelings, but also a drive to find out how others have coped.

While collecting this material, I've talked to dozens of widows, personally checked out social clubs and activities, searched for jobs and met with employment counselors, consulted psychologists and sociologists, anguished over my children's need for a father, and empathized with the difficulties other women face with their own families, friends, and finances.

I've ultimately survived, not because of my children, and certainly not because of any legacy, but because this cruel but not unusual trial by fire, this empty role known as widowhood, forces one to utilize all the material and psychological resources and to rely on a very bareknuckled, instinctive, and natural compulsion to be, to live.

Francis Bacon said, "Prosperity doth best discover vice, but adversity doth best discover virtue." Ironically, the archaic meaning of virtue is "manly excellence; valor." The phrase actually means: Adversity doth best discover strength. Because no matter how bad things have been for a widow—and they can be dreadfully, traumatically bad —if you can survive widowhood, then you'll emerge stronger, the best person you will ever be, without much help from your friends or family or the world out there.

This book is not meant to be merely a personal account of my own experience, nor is it an angry treatise on the injustice of our circumstances. Rather, by portraying a broad picture of widowhood, by presenting reports on individual approaches to what can only be called "survival," I hope to help my millions of sisters of all ages find strength and inspiration in the searches and solutions of their peers.

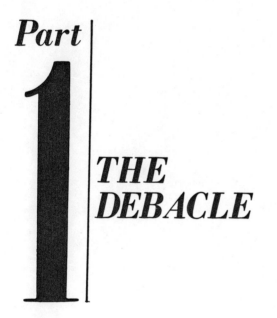

Part

1

THE DEBACLE

1 *Wife to Widow*

One minute you're a wife . . . and the next a widow. Maybe you saw this coming if your husband was one of the 20 percent of American men who die of cancer. Or one of the 10 percent who die of cirrhosis of the liver, as my husband did. For millions of women, that change in status occurs in a split second: a car accident or a fast and fatal heart attack (which causes 51.2 percent of all deaths).

The amount of time that elapses before death doesn't really make much difference, because nobody is quite prepared to be a widow. Even during terminal illness, one is still functioning as a wife.

And when death becomes a fact, there's not much time to reflect on your status. There are funeral plans to be made, friends and relatives to alert, children to deal with, a real sense of the immediate . . . and this is what saves you.

Based on the one major study done on widows in recent years—a comprehensive survey of 1,700 widows conducted by LIMRA, the Life Insurance Marketing and Research Association in Hartford, Conn.—psychologists conclude that there are three major phases of widowhood: impact, recoil, and recovery. Impact is described as the period of catastrophe (which can last from the moment of death to as long as six months later) in which "the full and direct effect of the initial stress is experienced . . . the widow restricts her field of attention, she seems stunned, she is unable to come to grips with what has occurred. Her time orientation is to the immediate *present*."

Some women have to be helped through this "impact" stage with drugs and/or fathers, brothers, friends they can lean on. Others get through it principally because they are in a state of shock. Before I became a widow, I marveled at the strength under grief of Jacqueline Onassis (then Kennedy), Ethel Kennedy, and Coretta Scott King. But when it happened to me, I realized that this was not so much grace as *shock*, which can also produce quite different reactions, such as the hysterically bereft behavior of other widows, including those both in and out of the headlines.

In discussing the impact stage of widowhood, psychiatrists have observed that "most women stay in character. If they are gracious, efficient hostesses, for example, they will be gracious and efficient during the period before and after the funeral."

I remember, in a kind of blur to be sure, calmly selecting the clothes Alex would wear during the wake, and culling through his favorite books for quotations he always loved which had some meaning to his life. I slept well that first night (I now realize it was exhaustion acting as a soporific), and the next morning I went down to my office and cleanly typed the poems and quotes so they could be offset and distributed to friends at the funeral.

I also remember being happy that on the day of the funeral the weather was pleasant, ordering liquor for the "party" afterward at our house, introducing cousins to friends, generating conversational topics of mutual interest, and even eating moderately well. Incidentally, my children behaved in a typical manner, too. It was only days afterward, or weeks afterward, that the reality set in for all of us, and quite a different set of behavioral patterns occurred, which we'll talk about in chapter three.

While this sense of the present, this immediate need to deal with a small, closed situation—that is, the funeral—propelled me to behave in a more or less "normal" fashion, the impact stage can produce quite different results.

Carole's reaction was that she could not, would not, accept the reality of her husband's death. It simply wasn't possible that her husband Jack had been killed in a stupid, careless car accident caused by a drunk, teenaged driver. She remembers nothing of the funeral, although she got through it without hysteria, and it is only now, two years later, that she can even talk about those first days and weeks. "That was a nightmare part of my life. There was no past. There was no future. And I couldn't accept the truth that the present meant my husband wasn't around. I was in a limbo where I seem to have functioned, but I honestly cannot remember how. We all just got through the days."

Irene, who now lives in San Diego, was widowed five years ago, at 37, when Peter died of a heart attack. They had been married thirteen years and the children were still babies (Cleo, 4½, and Randy, 2½). She remembers her initial reaction: "I talked feverishly with friends, tended to the business at hand with fierce authority, drank and took tranquilizers. I accepted the fact of Peter's death months, perhaps years, later. I will never know exactly when. During those first few days I shook. I shook a lot and I stared and could not sleep. I was in a state of absolute shock, but I functioned with some uncanny strength that emerged from God knows where. I was in absolute despair but cried very little in front of people. I acted brave. (Was I?) I cried alone, terribly.

"I went through the actions of taking care of the children but could not really pay them the attention they needed. I delayed telling Cleo for two days; Randy was too young to understand. I suppose I did everything to keep from appearing helpless. The most embarrassing fact: I was angry and outraged at death. I could not accept it gracefully. I believe the energy from the anger propelled me into action, almost immediately."

Noted columnist and author, Dr. Joyce Brothers, stresses the prevalence of this emotion. "Widows have a feeling of anger. They didn't expect this to happen to them. They are angry that they have been left. They are unrealistic. Shock affects them enormously, but unexpected anger is the hardest thing to accept."

The widows I've talked to agree that there is a significant difference in reaction when a husband dies after a long illness from when he dies suddenly. Perhaps this was illustrated most clearly by Lorraine, who has been widowed twice.

"The first time was really a shock because Jim died so suddenly, of a heart attack. He was only 48. I remember the funeral, but not much about it. My biggest worry was that my relatives were trying to give me sedation. I wouldn't take anything. I would make my own drinks or coffee to be sure they weren't slipping me something. Afterwards, I went back to work immediately."

In contrast, when her second husband died (they had been married about 2½ years, but he was ill for ten months of that time), "I was alone so much while he was in the hospital that I was prepared to be a widow again.

And also, the fact that I had gone through this before gave me more self-confidence and helped me get through it better. I knew what was ahead."

This sense of being prepared was echoed by Eve, whose husband had a history of heart disease ("I knew it was going to happen," she said) and Pat, whose husband died after a long fight with emphysema. Neither Pat nor Eve took any tranquilizers. They both found that going back to work was the medicine they needed.

Marilyn was widowed at 38 after seven years of marriage, but her husband had been in a hospital terminally ill with a rare disease similar to leukemia for two years. "So it wasn't a shock. But what amazed me was that although I had been functioning and competent for two years, when he died I became numb. I was numb through the funeral and for six months afterwards, when I sat and did nothing but work on my needlepoint. Luckily a good friend flew out to California to work out all the details of the funeral."

Helen had been trained in psychotherapy but had never worked privately until her husband died and she took over part of his practice. She observes, "A numbness sets in after the death that helps you to get through a difficult time. Call it shock if you will, but there is an emotional numbing that delays some of the pain. At the same time you find strength you never knew you had."

Although Helen had been very much the housewife for the eleven years she was married, when her husband became ill and then died, she changed: "It wasn't so much that I was calm, but I had a sense of having to take over. That was it. I felt I had to assume my husband's role. I handled the funeral, took the kids to the shore as we always did in the summer, wrote thank-you notes and entertained visitors. In retrospect, I'm impressed at how I managed. But at the time I just did what had to be done. I realize now that it's the everyday living later that's most difficult, not the special things related to the funeral."

Karen also remembers finding a strength she didn't know she had. "When the doctor came to sign the death certificate, he said, 'I hope you won't need any pills.' I looked at him, really surprised, because I may be the only person in this town, maybe the whole metropolitan area, who's never taken a tranquilizer, and I was not about to. I didn't drink, either. The day after Bob died, though, I went to the dentist with a really bad toothache, and for the whole next week that tooth really bothered me. Maybe that was a good thing. It got my mind off Bob."

Carla, who had been married for twenty years when her husband died in 1965, points out that the quality of the marriage dictates the degree of grief. "Remember, people marry for various reasons, not just love. Some widows are out hunting the day after the funeral, but these are the ones who originally married for money or social position. When you've married for love, dealing with the fact of death is nothing short of horrible."

Psychotherapist Martin Sylvester, Director of the New York Counseling and Guidance Service in New York City, feels that in most instances the important dynamic operative in why a widow doesn't fall apart immediately is all the attention she's getting. "The activity and confusion of a funeral, even the immediate aftermath when people are trying to sell you tombstones or insurance policies, is a kind of attention that diverts the widow from her real loss. But eventually these things fade, and relatives are not as much in evidence, and that's when depression hits. It's interesting to note that when a widow lives in an extended family group (with her parents or married children), she is less likely to fall apart."

In our society, the acceptance of death is as frightening as the idea of growing old. While there are many practical as well as questionable ways to stave off the advance of time, there is little psychological preparation for death and its aftermath for the people left behind who will suffer through the loss. Currently, thanatology (literally, the study of death) is gaining in popularity as a way of preparing the dying, and those who will survive them, for death. We are far from answers, however, or any comforting nostrums that make the actual event of death easier to take.

Our heads and our hearts have to rely on what is after all a very protective reaction—the shock of initial grief—to carry us through the debacle.

2 Battling the Bureaucracies and the Bill Collectors

The second phase of getting through the debacle is finding out where you are financially —usually a catastrophe in itself. For most widows this means an unending and bewildering barrage of frustrating contacts with lawyers, hospitals, banks, insurance companies, social security, the veteran's administration, credit card companies, and last but not least, the ghouls—the tombstone companies who are eager and persistent about erecting a monument to your dead husband.

Nanette Fabray, who became a widow after eighteen years of marriage to Ranald MacDougall, flatly declares, "Widowhood is a rip-off," and she names the impersonal attitude of banks, social security inequities, and government taxes as the greatest rip-offs. "Altogether, the government attitude is a criminal assault on the surviving mate."

15

Helen confided, "I was terrified about financial things; I had never handled them before. The car, the house, insurance, taking care of the bills. Everything had been perfect, just right; but when Paul died, there was this whole new world I had to take over in—and it was really trial by fire."

Sylvia Porter, the financial columnist, recently observed that after her father's death all her mother's inheritance, in stocks, was wiped out overnight in 1929. "It happened to lots of people, of course," she wrote in "Super-Sylvia" (*The Ladies Home Journal*, January 1976), "but Mother was absolutely ignorant about money. She was an object lesson in the mistakes widows make."

The mistakes—and the battle—begin immediately after the funeral, when you need money . . . and all your bank accounts are frozen. There is no point in talking about the "should have dones"—the importance of a will, knowledge of family investments, insurance, credit in the wife's name, not just the husband's, etc. And if your husband died suddenly, there was no time to withdraw money from savings or checking accounts. Although many widows with husbands who were seriously ill did receive good advice and made sensible arrangements, others were too busy dealing with his illness to coolly, calmly take care of financial affairs. So after the funeral you face a monetary bind.

In my own case, many kind friends sent checks instead of flowers, and at first I romantically thought I would use the money to set up a modest fellowship for writers (which Alex would have liked), but I quickly realized that he would also like to see his children fed and a roof over our heads. The money dribbled away in such day-to-day necessities, and within a month it was gone.

Fortunately, I had always earned money as a writer, and in a few short weeks I was back at the typewriter, working with a frenzy based on the need to live, which had little to do with creative drives.

If you talk to a dozen widows, or a hundred widows, you'll get as many different answers on this first attempt to work out the money crunch. Those who already had jobs reacted more or less in kind to my own behavior; those with readily converted insurance or pension plans had a different set of circumstances; and then there were a good proportion who had neither insurance, other annuities, nor jobs to fall back on. The LIMRA study reported that one widow in three said her family had no financial assets and that half had total liquid assets of less than $1,000.

Some local banks will be helpful in trying to assist you during this initial period when your funds are tied up, the will is being probated, or the insurance companies are slow in delivering. Others, as Miss Fabray pointed out, simply couldn't care less.

Jeanne had no difficulty because she was able to make arrangements in advance with her bank in Pittsburgh. "I had been in business with Dennis, and when he knew he was sick, he told our bank manager that I would be taking over. I borrowed money when I needed it, and I have a good credit reference. If I'm ever in a financial jam, I know I can go and talk to them personally and they will help."

The Estate

Troubles with the estate, as it's grandly called, vary in direct proportion to the size in question and whether or not there is a will. When I first started researching this book, I was shocked to discover that seven out of ten husbands die without a will. These figures were revealed in a recent survey conducted by Anchor National Financial Services, Inc., Phoenix, Arizona, and LIMRA and LUTC, two national life insurance associations. In talking to other widows, I realized that the figure had to be accurate—perhaps even on the low side. Interestingly, *all* of the widows I interviewed have wills and most have life insurance, including me.

When a husband dies intestate (without a will), it often means that any assets may be subject to litigation or to surprising legalities—in some states, the estate must be divided equally between children and wife. In addition, the widow may be forced to make financial arrangements and decisions under less than ideal circumstances.

In my own case, Alex left no will, but the only thing in his name *alone* was our 1966 Mustang, and since this was valued well under $5,000 (the ceiling for less complicated probate procedures in New Jersey), I did not have to buy back the car, but simply went to probate court and signed an affidavit on the amount of the estate that gave me title. I originally thought I would have no problem with the house because the mortgage was in both our names, but I soon discovered that what simplified matters was that our "estate" was under $120,000 and therefore not taxable.

When an estate is *over* $120,000, joint ownership of a house or property is not necessarily an advantage. Federal estate tax law assumes that all jointly owned property belongs to the first owner who died. When the husband dies, the value of the property is usually taxed from his estate. The law fails to credit a wife for equal ownership unless she can prove that she contributed to the purchase of the house or other property or paid an equal amount towards its upkeep and maintenance. (If she can prove such contributions, then the house would only be valued at half its worth for estate purposes.)

This has forced many a widow to sell her home or other property in order to pay off the federal taxes on the estate. Ironically, if the wife had died first, the husband would not be challenged on ownership. The E.R.A. is trying to equalize this position, but unfortunately the amendment has received such a bad press that the chances of it becoming part of our Constitution seem dim at this time.

In another twist on ownership problems when there is no will, one widowed friend had to buy back her own house at market value, using most of her insurance money, because the house had been mortgaged in her husband's name *only* and his family was making waves about the estate.

Ethel, a Michigan widow whose husband died in a car accident, was also devastated by the absence of a will. According to Michigan laws, the wife receives one-third of the estate; the children share the remaining two thirds, but it is held in trust until they are 18. In order to cope, Ethel had to sell a good deal of her farm property (which has been in her husband's family for over 100 years and is designated a landmark by the Michigan Historical Commission). She is supporting her young children on her one-third of the legacy by farming her own crops and renting some acreage. Ethel is also working toward a degree in home economics to help her manage her land and her finances more efficiently.

The situation may not be much better even in the three out of ten cases where husbands did have wills. According to syndicated writer Jane Bryant Quinn, wills are often drawn up by a lawyer and the husband with "arrangements they consider to be in (the wife's) best interests." All they need from her is a signature. And then after the death, these same women are asked to blossom as independent persons. Often the administration of the estate is under the jurisdiction of someone else (usually a male relative or a bank), so the widow is left with a feeling of not being trusted to manage her own affairs. Alan D. Bonapart, a San Francisco lawyer, points out that when this happens, "Widows become angry, even bitter, about the dependent lives they are forced to lead."

Life Insurance, Pensions, Annuities

This dependent situation also occurs in the dispensation of assets other than real property. Ellen reports that her husband was so sure she would marry again (and quickly) that he set up his life insurance benefits as a trust which would help his two daughters through college, but which released only a minimal amount of money to his wife to feed, clothe, and care for them in the meantime. "I'd be in really bad trouble if I didn't earn an income as a research assistant," she says.

Outsiders are inclined to overestimate the amount of insurance widows receive in general. The truth is that over half of all widows (52 percent) received less than $5,000 in life insurance proceeds. Even at the $15,000 income level, one widow in five had benefit payments of less than $5,000. The average widow received a little over $9,000 in life insurance payments.

Pensions, too, seem a likely souce for added funds for those whose husbands have died. Shockingly, only a small percent of American widows get any money at all from their husband's private industry pension plans, often because their husbands didn't realize they should apply for survivor's benefits . . . or because the pension was specifically engineered so that it would stop with the husband's death.

Getting It All Together

Unfortunately, there's no time after the funeral to wait for your emotional equilibrium to be restored before you must make crucial, often long-range decisions about your finances. At this point, "women are more apt than men to get the advice of a family friend or relative rather than get trained help," says Isabel Andrews, an account manager of Scudder, Stevens and Clark, a large investment counseling firm in New York. In "Seven Mistakes Women Make With Money" (*Money*, December 1975), a vice-president of The First Alabama Bank of Montgomery (which has fifteen branches with special divisions for women), agreed with Ms. Andrews and commented, "As soon as the funeral is over, all the family and neighbors assemble and the widow is subjected to a barrage of information, much of it wrong."

While professional help is in order, it is also true that many women who have never handled financial affairs are scared off by investment counselors who use highly technical language and can all too readily make you feel like some kind of fool. Roz Baron, an analyst with Dean Witter and Co. in New York, suggests going into a meeting armed with specific questions and, "if you do not understand what your advisor is saying, assume that it represents a failure on his part, not yours."

Often a lawyer or accountant can provide all the guidance you need if the estate is fairly small and uncomplicated. If there wasn't a will and you have minor children, for example, a lawyer would draw up papers appointing you guardian or custodian of any properties that might be theirs. (My lawyer drew up my will, with provisions for guardians if I should die, at the time we were straightening out the minor problems of Alex's estate.) You also need a lawyer and/or accountant to guide you with the odious, long-winded, difficult-to-decipher, IRS Form 706 which must be filed within nine months of your husband's death if the estate was over $60,000.

This is all role-changing time, of course, unless you are among the rather small minority of women who always handle the family financial affairs—or the even smaller minority who are thoughtfully included in the arrangements made by a husband to care for the family in his absence.

Social Security

Soon after the funeral, you'll come face-to-face with a seemingly beneficent institution—the Federal Government in the guise of Social Security. This is one area where outside advice is superfluous, because it couldn't possibly help you. "The fund" gets payment from 96 percent of all husbands, and therefore, as a widow, you and your children are entitled to your husband's benefits.

This sounds simple enough, but going through the social security spider web can make you forget your grief and take on the uncomfortable cloak of a Kafka-esque victim. Some of the wilder aberrations and inequities in this federal program are:

• You'll have to wait at least four months for your Social Security checks to start coming. Need money? Tough. As one bureaucrat told me, "You'll just have to go on welfare in the meantime." Kate waited six months! Fortunately she was working part-time. She immediately applied for and luckily landed a full-time job, but since she earns over $2,700 a year, she collects only $140.00 a month in Social Security benefits for her child.

• When your youngest child is 18 or stops going to college, you lose all Social Security benefits until you're 60.

• No matter how many children you have or how many years and how much your husband contributed to the fund, you'll only get a predetermined amount of money, which adds up to a maximum of 75 percent of the benefits your husband would have received had he lived. Irene has two children and receives $430.00 a month. If she earns over $2,700 a year, that amount will be cut in the ratio of $1.00 for every $2.00 she earns. When I talked to her I said I thought she was wrong because I had been told that if I earned over that amount, my benefits would *decrease*, but the children's would *increase* so that the $570 total we receive each month would be maintained.

After several calls to the Social Security office I discovered we were both right. Fortunately, because I have three children and am considered a family of four, an arbitrary need level, it would seem, we will always get "family maximum benefits" (until the children are 18, or through with college), no matter how much I earn. Irene, with her family of "three," loses out on income if she earns over the ridiculous, poverty-level $2,700 figure.

By the same token, if I had four, five, six, or more children, I would *not* receive more than that $570 limit.

• If you remarry, you lose your Social Security benefits, but the children will continue to receive them until they reach their majority or graduate from college.

• If you remarry when you're over 60, your checks will continue, but they may be reduced by as much as 50 percent. However, if this new marriage ends, your benefits will be reinstated.

Several widows I spoke with had had no problems with Social Security because they weren't aware they were entitled to any benefits. Deirdre, who has been widowed for ten years, never applied for Social Security, and though she manages well enough on her own income now, there were years when $255 or so a month would have helped her survive in expensive Houston. After our talk she decided to contact her local office to see if she might be entitled to any benefits.

Lorraine did check with Social Security and was appalled to discover that she would receive about $255 a month until she was 50—that's all. "I said to them, what if I'm sick or something. They told me to get a job, and I said what if I can't get a job, so they suggested welfare. Well, I do take care of myself, but because I earn over $2,700 a year, I receive nothing. The only time I'll benefit from Social Security will be when I retire—and then my own benefits will be greater than my husband's would have been."

As a stockbroker told me some years ago, before I could even begin to understand the truth of her statement and thought it was merely clever: "Social Security is neither social nor secure."

Blue Cross and Other Health Insurance Agencies

Not long after Alex died I received a bill from Englewood Hospital for $658.92. It took thirteen calls to the billing department before I was able to talk to anyone with any faint idea of what this was about. Incidentally, the thirteenth call was to the chief comptroller, and I learned that with any of these intricate billing systems one must go to the top—do not waste your time with clerks who don't return phone calls, misplace the files, or are either out to lunch or out on strike.

The comptroller told me this amount was for blood, a TV set (ridiculous since my husband was in intensive care), and a private room (ditto ridiculous), all items not covered by insurance. However, he couldn't tell me the corrected amount I owed because the computer only delivers this information on a once-a-month basis. He would, instead, send me a copy of the original print-out so I could figure out the mistakes myself.

Two days later I received a bulky envelope from the hospital: nine pages of computer-printed data with all expenses detailed on a day-by-day basis. On the last page the staggering total was $13,416.60—for twenty days of hospitalization (which did not include surgery).

Quaking, I called my friend the comptroller back who told me the bill had been paid by Blue Cross except for the $658.92. We struck out the TV set and the private room as errors, and I scrambled around to get the equivalent of $400.00 worth of blood. A few days later the comptroller called me with the news that Blue Cross was asking for their money back because a) the patient had *not* expired, and b) the autopsy reports hadn't been submitted—two reasons that seemed at cross purposes and definitely meant double trouble.

Subsequent calls established the fact that Alex had indeed "expired" and that the autopsy department had submitted a report (about 3 pages) which still hadn't been typed by the typists' pool—about one month after the autopsy!

At one desperate point I offered to type the damn report myself.

Finally Blue Cross honored their check, and, I thought, well that's solved. I didn't realize I was about to start a long-term, one-sided correspondence about paying the doctors' bills. While the hospital has some clout, the individual policy holder is braving it on her own in terms of doctor bills. My experience with Blue Shield was rather like throwing pebbles into the ocean . . . at most, a very minimal reaction.

Within one week after Alex's death (which occurred on the twenty-fourth of the month) I received neatly typed bills from all six attending specialists, addressed to the "Estate of Alexander M. Lindsay." The total bills amounted to about $1,600.00. I was in no position to pay these bills, but on good advice, I didn't even try. Instead I wrote letters to Blue Shield: explanations of our coverage, duplicate doctor's bills, death certificates, more duplicates of all of these. The correspondence was specifically ignored except for computerized notes reporting that the claims had all been rejected because of "insufficient information" or "this claim has already been paid," neither of which was true.

The breakthrough in my battle with Blue Shield came when the rank and file went on strike and I happened to reach an executive who was covering for the clerks. He followed through and eventually benefits were paid (ten months after the fact) for about 45 percent of the total bills. Too exhausted to fight on, I capitulated and am still paying the specialists—a little bit at a time—for the remaining balance. I must add, though, that in those ten months, two of the doctors sued me through medical collection agencies, a fact which did no good to my credit rating and very little to reinforce the theory that doctors are saintly creatures who, above all, are striving to preserve human life.

Nora, a St. Louis widow whose health insurance was not even used when Warren died of a heart attack, found it was cancelled immediately—just because. Marilyn, on the other hand, suffered through years of *no* Blue Cross/Blue Shield. She had no medical insurance, and in order to keep her paralyzed husband in the hospital and pay the monumental bills, she was forced to sell her paintings, jewelry, and any of the personal possessions she and Paul had acquired during their seven-year marriage.

The Veterans' Administration

The Veterans' Administration has a way of losing birth certificates, which means you will have to apply at least three times before getting the pension you are eligible for if your husband served in any branch of the armed forces. The only way to circumvent this is to send all letters registered mail. When that doesn't work, be sure you have at least four copies made of your children's and your own birth certificates, your marriage certificate, your husband's military discharge papers, and, of course, the death certificate to accommodate their clerical errors.

Do not become hysterical when you receive a letter directing you to fill out the attached form—which you've already filled out twice—and find the form is *not* attached!

Disability Payments/Unemployment Benefits

Follow the same formula as above. You are eligible for his disability benefits if your husband was working before his illness. In the case of unemployment, if he missed reporting days because of illness, you should get his back checks and then file a disability claim, but it will be a long, hard, frustrating fight.

Credit Card Companies

A book could be written on this subject alone—and should be written. My worst experience was with American Express. Alex and I had been equal partners in a public relations agency, Lindsay & Gray, and he had an American Express card based on the financial statement of the agency. I had never applied for a card in my own name; since we went everywhere together, it seemed a waste of the $10 or $12 annual membership fee. His card expired shortly after he expired, so I routinely applied for my card. Remember, I was a former full partner and now sole owner of the very company on which his credit was based. My application kept getting "lost"; I was referred to half a dozen toll-free numbers at American Express offices all over the country where sweet-voiced operators promised quick action. I finally called their legal department in New York and threatened to sue them with the help of the American Civil Liberties Union, a threat which then produced a card in my own name literally overnight. Incidentally, the A.C.L.U. told me that mine was a classic case of sex discrimination.

There are a couple of follow-up points on my AmEx experience that are amusing in a sour way. A week after I got my precious new card, I received a letter from the New Accounts Department which read, "Dear Ms. Lindsay: We are genuinely sorry that we cannot comply with your request for an American Express Card at this time . . . As much as we regret to decline an application, we are compelled to do so if it does not meet any one of the requirements . . . (When) you feel that your company's circumstances have changed, we cordially invite you to reapply."

It was also interesting that my new card was assigned a 900 AX number which I understand is the very worst credit line possible with this particular company. After I had the card a year, charged off my vacations, and paid the bills promptly, my new card the following year was given a 100 AX number. I guess by then my sex was forgotten and my faithful payments were rewarded with an upgrade in credit status.

When I told Marilyn this story, she was appalled, but admitted, "I wouldn't even have the courage to apply for an American Express card." Marilyn is self-employed as an interior decorator and therefore does not have a fixed income. I asked her whether her husband, a writer, who also didn't have a definite salary, had had an American Express card or Diners' Club card. "Of course," she said, and I think she now has the courage to apply for one.

When I asked Jill, who lives in Denver and was widowed at 36, if her charge accounts had been cancelled, she said, "Hell, yes," and specifically mentioned "(expletive deleted) American Express!"

Carla had a tussle over credit cards with the First National City Bank in New York, which had been her "neighborhood bank" for all her married years. "They sent me an application for a credit card and I filled it out, thinking it might be a good thing to have, even though I usually use cash. For over one year, I heard nothing about my application, even though I sent four or five notes and made quite a few phone calls. Finally I said to an officer, 'Look, I don't really give a damn about this now, but at least say yes or no.' I finally got my card."

As for the department stores, the sad but true fact of the matter is, don't ever inform them that your husband has died—leave all the cards just as they were or you'll find yourself with a wallet full of cancelled credit cards because now, as a widow, you are a bad credit risk . . . even though you have an income, even though you always paid your bills on time.

This theory is verified by one widow who moved from a northern California city to a southern area and tried to open new accounts in her own name. She was turned down because she had no "credit history." Her former accounts had been in her husband's name. Her job and savings were not viewed as reliable assets. She finally renewed the cards in her husband's name—even though he had been dead for seven years.

In Chicago, Kate had the same experience and still maintains her original credit cards, five years after her husband died.

Ironically, this kind of brouhaha over credit does not generally affect people who declare bankruptcy. Often they receive a handful of unsolicited credit cards—since they no longer "owe" any debts, they are now considered good credit risks.

Authorities urge widows and divorcees to establish credit in their own names. As Bess Myerson wrote, "(these) are the women who most often have to face the problem of no individual credit history, and at a difficult time, when the lack is one more added burden." It is crucial to open checking and savings accounts in your own name; then apply for credit cards, one by one—build a house of cards even if you don't intend to use them. For most of us there comes a day when we urgently *need* a credit file. You should have a line of credit at your bank —the maximum amount the bank will permit you to borrow against your account—and you can only establish this with some prior "approvals." As your credit history expands, the bank will proportionately increase your credit line—very necessary when you need to buy a new car, get a new air conditioner, borrow to send your kids to college.

Some credit problems will be solved by the Fair Credit laws which went into effect in October 1975. The Equal Credit Opportunity Act was designed primarily to aid women, and it forbids discrimination on the basis of sex or marital status. A companion bill, The Fair Credit Billing Act, provides uniform complaint procedures for credit-card holders. So far, according to an article, "New Fair Credit Laws Starting Smoothly," in *The New York Times* (November 13, 1975), not too many women are voicing their complaints. If you want fair treatment, make very loud noises; some of the places to take your troubles to—vociferously—are listed in Appendix IV.

But all is not equitable with the new credit bills, according to Ms. Myerson in her article "How to Fight for the Credit That Is Due You," in *Redbook* (September 1974). Although the Fair Credit Reporting Act gives a consumer the right to examine her credit file to find out why she's been turned down, if she has no credit history, there isn't a record for her to check! Furthermore, writes Bess, "in a neat Catch-22 that rubs salt in the abuse, with many credit bureaus, a husband's *bad* credit record follows both husband and wife, while a husband's *good* credit record follows only the husband. Heads they win, tails you lose."

The Tombstone Sellers

I have often said that if there were a scale of twenty or so jobs listed in descending order of preference, teaching school at a nursery or kindergarten level would be at the absolute bottom of my list (although I revere those dedicated ladies who have performed this Herculean task for all three of my kids). That dead last spot on the list has now been earned by those who make their living selling tombstones. Now I was very aware of the need for a tombstone for the grave, and I know everybody has to earn a buck, but these two considerations didn't make those frequent, sanctimonious and very irritating 7:30 P.M. calls from salesmen any more palatable. They are, after all, preying on your weakest points—your grief and your pride. But I finally became so angry that I told several salesmen in effect to "drop dead," a delicious pun I couldn't resist; that I would handle "the memorial" when I wanted to; and that, in the meantime, it was none of their business whether Alex had a "fitting" monument to his memory or not.

Eight months later I was able to calmly purchase a tombstone and the contract went to none of the people who had bothered me so prematurely.

3 | *The Real Thing*

Usually, at some point during your angry bouts with bureaucracies, but definitely immediately after, reality sets in. Shock is replaced by the real thing—grief in its most devastating form. This is one of the most difficult stages of widowhood because it's chiefly characterized by the knowledge of what isn't instead of what is.

Perhaps two or three months have gone by and you no longer mistakenly set the table for five instead of four; you're no longer setting out two coffee cups in the morning or ordering too much meat from the butcher. After a period of blurred day-to-day living, a limbo in which getting through each twenty-four-hour period is a minor miracle, you know finally, really, and awfully that your husband is dead. You accept the fact that you won't hear the garage door shut at night any more and hear his steps on

33

the stairs. You'll be the only adult closing that door or climbing those stairs.

The psychologists working on the LIMRA study call this phase of widowhood *recoil*, "the time when the widow achieves her first full awareness of what has happened, and there is a period of personal turmoil as she realizes the changes that have taken place. The first real, overt expression of emotion comes during this time. The widow is oriented and preoccupied with the past."

Although no one can pinpoint when this stage begins and ends, there is general agreement that a traumatic series of changes takes place: coping with overwhelming grief and loneliness, periods of guilt and self-blame, real and hysterical fears, dangerous confrontations with stress, searching for solutions to calm these conditions.

The widows I talked to had experienced the total spectrum of grief from immediate awareness of what had happened to a delayed reaction. Kate was widowed at 36 after thirteen years of marriage when her husband committed suicide. Now 42, she recalls, "Reality set in after the funeral was over and I went home to an empty house." Aside from grieving over her own loss, she felt a different kind of sadness. "The person who dies is always alone. Your feeling of grief is that you couldn't really be with that person, couldn't share his grief at having to die."

For Beth, the real awareness of her tragedy came about six months after. "The toughest times are evenings and weekends, especially in the beginning." "Bereaved," after all, means to be robbed of a life. The surviving partner has had a companion stolen, snatched away, and the void is awesome.

Helen, who is also a social worker, says, "Nobody dies for you at the moment of death. You don't really give up the person until quite a time afterwards. Of course, when there is a long illness involved, some widows give up the person, consider him dead *before* the actual death. Basically, though, somebody doesn't die in your unconscious when they die. If you notice, probably your dreams are not about Alex being dead, but of him as alive. I daydream about my husband as being alive, but not paying attention to me."

Daydreaming was an important way for me to sidestep this confrontation with reality, and it took a long time to accept facts and not fairy tales. Sometimes I'd lie in bed in the morning, half asleep, half awake, and think that maybe this was just an over-long dream. A dream that lasted for two months, six months, eleven months. But then after about a year, I couldn't work up that fantasy anymore, and I knew this was no dream. It was real and Alex would never be coming back.

Nora, whose husband died two years ago, told me, "I thought the finality of death came through immediately, but of course it didn't. Sometime during the following year I was able to accept the reality. Looking back, it was probably after attempts at dating and sex failed, plus the exhaustion of dealing with four children alone. The long evenings would stretch forever, and the repetition of aloneness made it final."

In an essay called "Accepting the Fact," the late Marvin Goldfine, who was Jewish chaplain at New York's Columbia Presbyterian Medical Center, wrote, "Acceptance of the fact of death does not come easily, but no return to normal functioning is possible until it has been accomplished. Upon it depends one's ability to make the proper adjustments in his mode of life. What is virtually at stake is the achievement of a new balance in one's orientation to reality."

Lorraine's realization that her first husband was dead was immediate: "I don't agree with the psychologists. I had a feeling of pure pain. I knew it with a thud, a crash.

I knew what had been my life was over."

No matter when the real grieving hits, this stage will be flooded by gallons of tears.

In his booklet, "On Being Alone" (see Appendix I), Dr. James A. Peterson, of the Gerontology Center at the University of Southern California in Los Angeles, says, "No one cries very much unless something of real worth is lost. In a sense, grief and despair are the measures of loss. They are testimonials to the value of that which is gone."

We widows, then, are deluged with "testimonials."

This is the time when you burst into tears in the strangest places: the supermarket, during your son's piano lesson, at a P.T.A. meeting, or in a restaurant waiting to have lunch with a friend. Terry, a fifty-one-year-old Boston widow who lost her husband a week after their twenty-fifth anniversary, said, "Afterwards, for a few months I wouldn't wear mascara because I never knew when I'd cry, and the crying was bad enough, but you don't want to look like a damn fool with black stuff all over your face. It's funny that you can be that sad, but that organized."

Eve, widowed at 46 after seventeen years of marriage, remembers crying when she was home alone after leaving friends, and Pat, who had always enjoyed her own and her husband's large and close family, found herself crying at family gatherings.

Rose, who became a widow at 32, with a two-year-old son, remembers crying a lot while her husband was ill for a year (with nephritis), and then afterwards when she was job hunting or short of funds (which was often). This peppy lady, who happens to be my great-aunt, is now 65 and has been a widow for thirty-three years, but one of the events that made her cry most was the loss of all her personal possessions, right after her husband died. She had to leave her home and move in with her parents, and since she had no money, she prevailed on a friend to move her furniture and clothes and household things. On the way to her parents' home, the truck caught fire and everything was destroyed. Aside from the emotional trauma, the truck wasn't insured for this kind of damage and Aunt Rose found herself literally with nothing!

Irene recalls "crying a lot at unexpected times: when I woke up, in the car on the way to the grocery store, when I had to do something as simple as fix dinner. Thank God the children provided a distraction, because they demanded my attention constantly, and also, within two months, we moved from New York to San Diego and this kept my mind off how rotten I felt."

This is the time when you are completely exhausted, but can't sleep, the time when you lose weight, because you're too nervous to eat, or gain weight because you're too nervous *not* to eat. (Significantly, the word "companion" literally means "one with whom you break bread.")

Eating was a definite problem with all the widows I talked to, but there was a higher percentage of women who could not eat than those who swallowed their grief with food. Jeanne describes her experience as being very bad at first. "I couldn't cook for myself, but eventually I knew that if I didn't do this, I'd get sick, so I made myself prepare a real dinner, which I then had to eat. I set the table, and really forced myself to eat. But now, after my second widowhood, I don't do that, I'm much more casual about it and eat out more or fix something simple."

In my own case, Alex and I always ate after the children; it was a quiet, special time for us. Now, although I do cook a good meal for them, the idea of sitting down at a table by myself is impossible, so I usually fix scrambled eggs or a sandwich and eat while I'm reading the paper or watching TV. Helen follows much the same routine, while Anita, Adelle, and Anne, who either have no children (or none at home) and work during the day, find that the best answer is to have a good meal at lunchtime and just a light snack in the evening.

There is an awareness, though, and fear of getting ill because of bad eating habits that concern all of us. Pat says, "In the three years my husband was sick, I lost over thirty pounds, and after he died I really made an effort to build myself up. I knew I'd be alone from here on in, and there was nobody around to take care of me."

Nobody around sums up this period of widowhood because, most of all, this is the time when you experience real loneliness, which is very different in kind from that of the first few months. Now the sounds of silence are what destroy you. For me, there is no typewriter clacking away in the next room in a kind of rhythm with mine. Also, Alex snored, a bane of my life all during our marriage— but what I would give *now*, to be awakened by that cacophany, to have someone to punch (gently, of course) so he would stop snoring, instead of pounding a pillow every night trying to fall asleep.

At night, after the children are in bed, you start talking to yourself because there's no one else to talk to. By this point friends have grown weary, or perhaps wary, and are inclined to offer "stiff-upper-lip" advice. You make ill-advised phone calls at midnight or later, and can hear the heavy resignation on the other end of the line.

Marilyn had always enjoyed solitude, "so it wasn't that there was one special time I couldn't stand to be alone. But like you, my husband worked at home and we had a twenty-four-hour-a-day relationship. He was always home. At first the entire day seemed empty and for two years I went through the most catastrophic kind of loneliness."

What Adelle misses most are Sunday brunches with her husband, which were something special. "We always used the crystal and silver, and good china, and a linen tablecloth, and I would make something unusual and gourmet-ish. It was really our day, and after brunch we did whatever we wanted to: sometimes nothing, or just reading the papers all day long. I still haven't been able to use any of my nice things, because they remind me of Dan and our Sundays together."

You begin to think you're actually going crazy; you're beset by feelings of guilt, a variety of illnesses (which are either psychological, or hypochondriacal, but illness, nonetheless), a good dollop of anger—yes, anger--at those who are "luckier" than you, or don't understand your situation, and a very frightening sense of being all alone. You know that your life has drastically, irrevocably changed.

In an unheralded, but very interesting book, *Religion and Bereavement*, Edgar N. Jackson, D.D., Chairman of the Advisory Board of the Guidance Center of New Rochelle, New York, writes, "It is important to realize that grief has the characteristics of a neurosis . . . Physically, these symptoms may include shortness of breath, a choking sensation, sighing, and crying, sometimes to hysterical proportions. Symptoms may also include nausea, loss of appetite, loss of sphincter controls or compulsive eating and drinking, weakness of the large muscle system, dizziness, faintness, and an overall feeling of distress. All are quite normal and nothing to be alarmed about if they do not persist over a lengthy period."

When experiencing these symptoms, which are, after all, *abnormal*, if viewed in the light of how you feel and behave ordinarily—in your old life—it is difficult, if not impossible, to be as clinical about it. A "this-too-shall-pass" philosophy offers very little reassurance.

Time for a New Role

Aside from the physical reverberations, the new status as widow has far-reaching psychological dimensions. Mrs.

Diana Horowitz, Director of the now-defunct Widows'
Consultation Center in New York City, describes this
period of awareness as a time "when the widow is suddenly faced with rejection on all sides. This serves to reinforce her sense of worthlessness. Society has provided
nothing and our churches are very remiss, although some
have formed widows' groups. In working with close to
2,000 clients, only a handful of people said they got any
help from their clergymen."

In a paper published in *The Family Coordinator*
("Helping Widows: Group Discussions as a Therapeutic
Technique," Volume 24, July 1975, Number 3), S. Roxanne Hiltz (Ph.D.) adds, "The problem of finding a new
identity is also very emotion-laden because it involves giving up one's old identity as a wife." One group leader
described this trauma: "When the person is alone, here
she is having invested so much psychic energy into the
partner . . . 'No, no, no, I'm still a wife. No, no, no, I'm
still nothing. No, no, no, I don't have to find things out
for myself. No, no, no!' "

As sociologist Robert Fulton said at a conference on
widowhood at Harvard, "What must be faced by the survivor is the fact that in a very real way, she is confronted
with a spoiled identity; as survivors we are stigmatized by
the death of the ones we love. With one person out of
every twenty a widow or widower, the problem is neither
irrelevant nor inconsequential; it is a very serious social
problem with profound psychological overtones for us
all."

When you married, you chose to assume a role, and the
same was true when you became a mother, a parent. But
now a new role is thrust on you and adjusting to it is
something less than easy. Estelle, who was widowed at
thirty-eight with a girl, 8, and a boy, 4, says, five years
later, "I still feel like half a person." She finds it difficult
to relate to her neighbors, her family, her children. "I re-

ally don't know who or what I'm supposed to be."

Another characteristic of this role is that you feel empty, unfulfilled. There is nobody to give yourself to on an adult level, mentally or physically. JoAnne said, "The children don't count. Although I'm giving them a slightly different view of me, I'm still their mother. But I'm nobody's wife. And I was used to being a wife for sixteen years."

There was another curious development in terms of role-playing that happened to me and other widows with parents on the scene. We reverted to being children again. Not necessarily because we wanted to (although this situation is discussed in chapter four), but because our parents saw us in this framework. When there was a husband in evidence, we daughters were "grown-up, equal, capable of functioning." Remove the husband and you reincarnate a dependent daughter. The mother of one widow, who was herself a widow, told me, "Oh my poor Harriet, I feel so sorry for her, I don't know how she manages. I go over and cook dinner for her three or four times a week because it's so difficult with the children." If Harriet's husband were alive, Harriet would be cooking dinner anyway, but to her mother, she isn't able to perform this routine function as adequately anymore. She's a child once again. When her mother said this, Harriet only raised an eyebrow, but later she added her own opinion. "Mom means well, but sometimes she causes more confusion with her constant worries about us. I'm grateful for all her help and I don't want to hurt her feelings, but even the boys get tired of eating her specialties and ask me to make their own favorites."

The Verdict: Guilty

Another booby trap in your early days as a widow is the sinking feeling of guilt. *Guilt!*

I have spent my professional life writing about health

and vitamins and how to take care of your body. Why didn't I realize what was happening to Alex? Why couldn't I call in better doctors, move him to a different hospital, avert what had happened to him, *stop* him from dying? Well, now I realize there was nothing more I could do, but I went through a period of self-recrimination that most of us have to experience. This is what psychologists term "short-lived guilt." "If we hadn't gone to the party . . ." "If I had only seen that he was looking ill . . ." "If I hadn't had that fight with him . . ." "If I hadn't pushed so for a new car . . ." "If I had only *known*."

Well, we didn't know, and even if we did, it's unlikely we could have prevented what happened. But now we're here, and he isn't, and we have to deal with, assuage, wipe away the guilt. Dr. Peterson says, "There are some persons who are so insecure that they attribute every problem . . . to their own inadequacies. This is unfair to themselves, but it is often such a deep-rooted feeling that long talking with a kind friend or counselor is necessary to eliminate that type of self-blame."

Only Fear Fear Itself

Another role in this drama is that old "devil" *fear*— and he wears a lot of hats. One of them is the fear of being alone, in terms of security. After Alex died I was super-cautious about locking windows, the garage door, the car, none of which I had bothered about when he was alive. We live in a fairly quiet and safe neighborhood, and while we don't leave our doors open at night, we were never so clutched up about security.

I asked my father to put a chain-lock on the front door; I put a padlock on the gate to the back yard. I was petrified. But after a few months I realized most of the world out there doesn't know that I'm a poor, defenseless widow. Ostensibly, our life here at home continues just as it was. Who could know there wasn't a husband in residence? But still, having reached this sensible viewpoint, I have instructed the children never to say their father is dead when some dumb insurance agent calls for Alex, or someone is trying to sell us a bungalow in the Poconos. When I call plumbers or electricians I never reveal my single status. I'm still Mrs. Alexander Lindsay. And although I may flinch when the plumber says, "Your husband could do this," I make no comment . . . and then try to do the mechanical task myself.

I have also memorized the number of the local police, something I hadn't done in the twelve years I lived in this town before Alex died.

But there's another type of fear that confronts widows: the fear of spending the rest of our lives alone. This is quite different from being lonely. We are talking about an existential type of aloneness. We were born alone and we'll die alone, and widows and widowers, more than other people, recognize this. The harsh reality is that we may have to spend the next twenty or thirty years without a man to share our lives, bring up our children, manage or help manage our money, love, and have sex with. And this is a very real fear which you can't lock doors against, or call the police department about. Having opted some time ago to go through life with a partner, it is a fearsome, scary development to realize you may be alone . . . forever.

Dealing with Stress

There is a current theory that the majority of the illnesses of recent twentieth-century life are caused by stress: the pressures of job, money, love will do most of us in. Well, possibly your husband was a victim of this malady (and I think my husband was), but what is more important for you and me and the rest who are left is the power stress has over *our* lives now. On the face of it, the prognosis is not good.

In his report, "That Helpless Feeling: The Dangers of Stress," in *New York* magazine (July 14, 1975), Douglas Colligan concluded that based on his interviews with leading scientists and physicians, "Intense feelings of helplessness can lead to more than mere physical disease; loss of control of one's life can end in loss of life itself."

● Dr. Samuel Silverman, Associate Clinical Professor of Psychiatry at Harvard Medical School, reported that in twenty years of practice, he's observed that "if a psychological manifestation of distress (such as guilt, grief, or rage) suddenly disappears, the trouble usually surfaces again at the body's weakest point, the target organ." In addition, there is often "somatic identification," when a person develops a similar ailment to one suffered by a mate.

● Dr. Arthur Schmale of Rochester wrote a paper entitled "Giving Up as a Final Common Pathway to Changes in Health." Based on a survey of hospitalized patients, he found grief to be one of the most common causes for what he labels the "giving-up complex." One British survey, ominously called the "Broken Heart Study," showed that 4,500 widowers studied within six months of the deaths of their wives had a 40 percent higher mortality rate than other men their same age.

● Dr. George Engle, part of a group researching stress at the University of Rochester School of Medicine and Dentistry, catalogued eight different causes of sudden death in a file of 170 cases. Among the most common causes was a "tremendously intense emotion such as grief coupled with feelings of helplessness."

Drs. T. H. Holmes and R. H. Rahe, in their article, "Longitudinal Studies of Life Change and Illness Patterns" (*Journal of Psychosomatic Research*, 1967), rated varying amounts of stress brought about by specific changes in the lives of 5,000 of their patients. Their findings indicate that the more stressful the changes, the more likely a person was to suffer or develop some serious stress-related illness in the next few years, including heart disease, menstrual disorders, migraine headaches, asthma, skin ailments, digestive troubles, and ulcers.

According to their studies, if you accumulate 200 to 300 stress points over a twelve-month period, you have more than a fifty-fifty chance of becoming seriously ill in the next few years. I took the test myself and came up with the following results:

Life Event	Value Rating
Death of a spouse	*100*
Sex difficulties	*39*
Business readjustment	*39*
Change in financial state	*38*
Change in number of arguments with spouse	*35*
Mortgage over $10,000	*31*
Change in living conditions	*25*
Revision of personal habits	*24*
Change in recreation	*19*
Change in sleeping habits	*16*
Change in eating habits	*15*
Christmas	*12*

Total: 393

Although I'm still alive, but hardly kicking, I am nonetheless troubled by my vulnerability. Dr. William A. Nolen, author of *The Making of a Surgeon*, wrote in a recent article, "Stress and How to Live With It," in *McCall's* (April 1975), "Whichever organ or system in your body is weakest by nature will be the one that gives you trouble when you're under stress." In this vein, Beth, whose husband died of a heart attack, reports that she had the same symptoms he had. "I had sharp heart pains, especially when a man wanted too much from me in a serious way. I went through depression and tiredness for two years. The happy times tended to be manic. I smoked too much, and I was ill too many times with chronic bronchitis."

On a more up-key note, Dr. Jerome Singer, co-author of *Urban Stress*, says, "People adapt to most stresses they face. Things which are at first too unpleasant to bear become less and less so over time and eventually get to be a routine part of normal life."

Ever the optimist, he suggests a five-part program for reducing stress: relaxing, emphasizing the beneficial results of certain stressful situations, arranging a schedule so that stress occurs predictably, setting up situations so that stress can be controlled, and avoiding the postponement of moderately stressful situations. None of this does much good for widows except his advice about relaxation, and that I'm afraid is easier said than done.

For Malvina Douglas, whose husband Kenneth Douglas (a noted editor and writer) was killed in a freak accident in 1975, an interest in Eastern philosophy helped her deal with stress. She took no drugs or tranquilizers, but relied on meditation. In one of her articles she wrote that accepting life's crises is only possible if "I can recognize through meditation the impermanence of all material and living things in the world and can accept this as well as understand the fullness of the One-ness of us all." The depth of her grief is underlined by her explanation, "How can I tell you how beautiful a marriage we had. He was my friend, my guru—everything."

Drugs, Alcohol, and Other Panaceas

I never understood why my widowed aunts seem to dote on Valium, but when I became one of the group, albeit quite younger, the value of Valium was crystal clear. It's all very well to be brave, and we spend a lot of our time being brave, but if anyone raises a condescending eyebrow about a widow's weakness in relying on Valium to fall asleep, I challenge them to live through one week of sleepless nights before they come around to "our" side. There are various ways of getting through the days, and I will describe dozens of them, but the nights, the nights. Now I understand what the phrase "bête noir" really means. Irene remembers routinely "popping two or three Miltowns—I was frantic for sleep."

Of course, one does not want to be a victim of what *Ms.* magazine calls "misogynist ads," which depict women as neurotic weaklings. Yet stories you read about the dangers of relying on Valium or other tranquilizers are always so breezy in suggesting that one should solve problems in stronger, more positive directions, through counseling, let's say, or by taking direct action. The authorities who blab on most gustily are those who don't seem to have the problems in question.

In their article "Do You Take Valium?" (November 1975), *Ms.* reported that "many psychiatrists regard anxiety as 'normal'—a necessary pre-condition to solving problems. Valium, they say, is simply the most popular way of managing rather than mastering difficulties." And it is popular. Approximately 15 percent of the U.S. population takes Valium. It is the largest selling tranquilizer, the most widely prescribed drug in the world.

Other psychiatrists are up on tranquilizers and find they are needed to bolster confidence in the ability to cope. Despite this general disagreement between the two

factions, all doctors concur that there is an alarming pre-
disposition toward overprescribing Valium and the like
for every little emotional twinge.

The trouble is that Valium is a drug that acts on the
central nervous system, and as it is with most of these
drugs, after a while you get hooked on them . . . and
after a while it takes more to achieve what just a little bit
of Valium did at first. One is inclined to soup up the dos-
age. There have also been some recent studies indicating
that after long-term usage Valium, even in modest
amounts, can produce effects quite opposite from those
which were desired: insomnia may replace sleepiness, nervousness may result instead of tranquility. And then, too,
even small doses have been known to cause fatigue, nausea, slurred speech, staggering gait, headaches, disorienta-
tion, and so on.

Valium is, after all, a mood-altering drug, and in the
beginning, this is just the medicine many widows need. In
a few months, though, try to ease off on it. Although you
may not be able to sleep at first, eventually you will.
When you find yourself taking that little yellow pill (or
one of its sisters), just *in case* you don't sleep, it's time for
you to either kick the habit or talk to your doctor. My
own self-imposed rule now is to go to bed at night without
taking one, but if I wake up at 3:00 or 4:00, I don't spend
the next hours tossing and turning (I do have to get up
with the children at 7:30). I take half of the 5-milligram
pill and sleep through the rest of the night. But now I find
that I have to do this less and less often.

A stiff scotch on the rocks or a brandy can also help
anesthetize one enough to get through the nights . . . and
in some cases, the days. The latest figures show that there
are 800,000 women alcoholics, the majority of whom are
not women who live alone. But how can they tell? How
can they judge or estimate the amount of drinking that

goes on behind the closed doors of quite respectable widows, divorcees, and other single women?

About 20 percent of the widows I interviewed were against relying on tranquilizers or alcohol for solace. Vera, widowed with five children, age 13 to 2, and in an absolute financial mess that was further entangled by a will written before her marriage, prefers to go it alone. "Tranquilizers and the rest are crutches that a widow may or may not need to get through intensely distressing days. But the problem is many widows begin to feel justified about their dependency on these crutches, and that leads to self-destruction. You'll have to do away with any of these supports sooner or later if you are going to survive."

Tina, who had been married nineteen years, admits, "During the first year or so I was drinking too much, and in my experience, all widows I've known do this. I think one reason is you are making an effort to be attractive socially, to be on; it's not so much that you're drinking to forget your troubles, but to gear up, rev up for a social occasion that's after all, difficult at the beginning."

Nancy had been married to Ken for ten years. It was her second marriage, and when he died she was desperately unhappy. "At first I drank, I smoked, I took tranquilizers, I was a zombie, although outwardly functioning. Then my doctor set me straight on the drinking and the pills—although I still smoke furiously. So I stopped escaping that way and I walked. I walked for six months. Sometimes I'd walk twenty miles a day, in all types of weather. And then I'd get home so exhausted I didn't need pills or a drink. All I needed was sleep, and I slept."

Karen has always had the habit of staying up very late, which turned out to be an advantage. "I've always done this. I wander around reading or watching TV until I'm really sleepy, and then when I get into bed I fall asleep quickly."

Other ways of dulling the reality? Some widows find what they miss most is cuddling . . . and so they find someone, anyone, to cuddle with (it's the body presence that comforts). Others work so hard at their daytime activities that they fall immediately into sleep at night— troubled, tossing sleep, but sleep in any case.

In his upbeat book, *How To Survive the Loss of a Love* (Lion Press, 1976), co-author Peter McWilliams included one of his poems that I found particularly apt:

> *although my*
> *nature is not to*
> *live by day*
>
> *I can not*
> *tolerate another*
> *night like this.*
>
> *so*
>
> *I will wake-up*
> *early*
> *tomorrow morning and*
> *do do do*
> *all day long,*
>
> *falling asleep*
> *exhausted tomorrow*
> *early evening,*
> *too tired*
> *even for*
> *nightmares.*

The Need to Talk

For some reason, although American women have been conditioned to listen to friends talk about troubles with husbands, sex-life, money, children—the most intimate subjects—there's a taboo on talking about your dead mate. As one psychologist said, "Our society wants everyone with a problem to talk about it . . . except widows."

Jane Seskin, a writer who was widowed at a very early age in a reverse version of *Love Story*, is trying to change public attitudes about dying, but she admits, "This isn't easy. People don't want to talk about death."

This was also the experience of another writer, Geraldine Palmer, whose husband died of cancer after a one-week illness, plunging Geraldine and her two young children into bewildered grief. Not only did people not want to talk about it, but "they didn't believe me," she writes in *Singles World* (March 1976). "They couldn't feel or understand my pain, my bewilderment, and my abject grief. Not my parents, my brother, my friends, relatives, nor psychiatrist."

Millie found herself specifically *not* discussing how lonely she felt. "Before I was widowed I had a friend who lost her husband, and she was always depressed, always crying. Finally I started to avoid her because it was depressing me. I said to myself then—and this seems so strange now that it eventually happened to me—'If I'm ever in that situation, I must not do this because it's not fair to other people and you just lose the friends you have.' "

On the other hand, Sarah, an attractive 39-year-old who was known for her big-hearted sympathy, told me, "I wanted to talk to someone about Hal, not to be sad, but to remember some of the good times we had together. But after a couple of months, friends weren't calling me, or if they did, they'd say a tight little 'how are you,' which I knew meant I was supposed to say, 'I'm okay, we're doing alright.' Finally I made a list of the friends I'd listened to and I said to myself dammit, it's time they listened to me. But I really didn't find the phone calls very satisfying."

The problem with this kind of contact is that you are likely to make the calls at 1:30 at night when totally depressed, or after having two drinks instead of one, or when it's your anniversary or your husband's birthday.

Joanne said, "I'm a man's woman. I don't dig the idea of rehashing these problems with a bunch of grieving widows. So rather than talk to them, when I started going out with men, I managed to nip most relationships in the bud by telling them the sad saga of my life on our very first meeting—which often turned out to be the last."

But it's crucial to be able to talk—to give vent to one's grief—and if you can't talk to friends, and you can't talk to your minister or priest or rabbi, then try to track down a widow's rap group. More and more of them are forming all over the country.

The first psychiatrically backed group of this type was organized in 1964 by widowed Dr. Phyllis Rolfe Silverman, Ph.D., while she was working at Harvard Medical School. The Widow-to-Widow Program (see Appendix II) was sponsored jointly by a local synagogue, a YMCA, a Catholic women's organization, and The Laboratory of Community Psychiatry. The emphasis was on coping with the untimely death of a spouse in young families.

In an analysis of the program (which continues after twelve years), *Mental Hygiene* (July 1969) reported, "Statistics show that young widows and widowers have a proportionately greater risk of needing treatment for an emotional disorder than would be expected from their numbers in the population."

Dr. Silverman started her program because her talks with widows revealed that the majority felt that the people who could help them most effectively were *other widows* —not their families, doctors, or clergymen, who were predominantly anxious for them to recover quickly and offered "stiff-upper-lip" advice. (LIMRA, The Life Insurance Marketing and Research Association, impressed with the results of the Boston program, tried to initiate other widow-to-widow programs across the country, but were unable to do this on a nationwide scale because "widows are not a popular cause.")

There is, however, a nationwide group which has been quite successful and was developed by another widow, Bea Decker, whose three children were quite young when she was widowed sixteen years ago. Bea, who is co-author of a very moving book, *After The Flowers Have Gone* (see Appendix I), founded THEOS—a Christian fellowship for young and middle-aged widows and widowers. THEOS relates not only to the Greek word for God, but stands for "They Help Each Other." When she started the program in the early sixties, it was very informal in scope and was based in her hometown of Penn Hills, a suburb of Pittsburgh. Today there are over thirty chapters in California, Florida, Illinois, New Jersey, Ohio, Oregon, Pennsylvania, Texas, and Canada (see Appendix II).

Bea says, "Tears are prayers. Tears are healing. They are a process you must go through. Don't be afraid to grieve. The grief must be worked through, and the worst mistake is to rush into re-marriage to escape loneliness . . . Unresolved and unexpressed (grief) can only give birth to an emotional cripple. But so often the griever weeps alone! Grief does not fit into our way of life, nor do its victims. Modern society has no time for death, and since the griever is a reminder of death, he stands alone."

THEOS tries to provide support, companionship, and comfort with monthly rap sessions and lectures on loneliness, legal matters, children, finances. Perhaps even more important is the one-to-one basis of peer help available through their twenty-four-hour telephone "hot-line."

The need for direct communication and the ability to talk over the problems was also pinpointed by Helen Antoniak, the widowed director of the Widowed-to-Widowed Program in San Diego (see Appendix II). Helen also runs a hot-line, writes a newsletter, and tries to assist widows in California and other areas around the country who want to form their own person-to-person programs. In a letter to one new widow, Helen wrote, "I know it is tough to be outgoing and seek new friends, but the consequences of not doing it are drastic. We all need at least one person we are not afraid to call at 2:00 A.M."

Joyce had the same goals. She started an Outreach Program in New Haven after her husband died to share the problems and provide solace. She says, "When I encounter someone newly bereaved, I know I'm helpless. There is nothing I can do to make the person come back. I can only be a listener."

In Chicago, Barbara also wanted to help other widows avoid what she had experienced. Her policeman husband was shot and killed when she was only 27, in 1967. Her major problem with widowhood was not financial (she received a pension and continued working at her job), nor was it loneliness—her family and friends were there for company. "The one thing I didn't have that I really needed was a friend to unburden myself on, someone who had been through it herself, someone to talk to, someone I wouldn't be afraid of upsetting with my pain because she knew first-hand."

Barbara married another police officer several years ago, but she hasn't forgotten the widow's need to talk. She is currently president of the Chicago Police Wives Association (which has almost 1,000 members), and has worked out a widows' trust fund, a police family assistance fund, and a widows' assistance program for police widows. Most important, she has made sure that there is always someone around to listen when a widow has to express her grief.

While many rap groups are directed and conducted by lay persons (widows, all), others have the support and help of professional therapists. In Dr. Hiltz's paper on the "late" Widows Consultation Center, she writes that the once-a-week sessions with groups of widows were led by psychotherapists. "It takes very special skills to be able to lead a group of bereaved women in discussions that will be constructive, rather than depressing or upsetting."

The value of professional help is echoed by the Reverend J. Donald Bane, Director of the Sound Counseling Center in Harrison, New York. "Widows and widowers must be able to express feelings of grief," he says. "We're too afraid of feeling helpless. Let the person be angry or hurt, but be able to go through these emotions with him."

None of these organized groups are designed as social clubs (although there are others which we'll discuss in chapter eight that have dual purposes). At THEOS, for example, the ratio of women to men at their meetings is ten to one, almost exactly in keeping with the ratio of widows to widowers. Eleanor Lubin, President of the Jewish Widow-Widowers Club (see Appendix II) in Belmont, Mass., a surburb of Boston, says, "We do *not* even attempt to be a 'dating' or 'matching' group. We do have some male members but they are usually greatly outnumbered by females, and our emphasis is on us all as *people*."

Some widows are inhibited by the idea of group sessions and would prefer to talk out their troubles on a one-to-one basis of professional counseling by psychologists. Kate found this to be helpful in her case when she started family counseling several years ago because of a crisis with her brain-damaged daughter (now 15), and she is still in therapy.

Once more, psychiatrists have not reached agreement on which type of counseling is most rewarding. Some feel that "immediate crisis intervention" by professional therapists is called for to help adults and children. Others, like Dr. Silverman, feel that self-help groups, widows helping other widows, are most beneficial.

And there is still one more point of view, put forth by Dr. Herbert Holt, author of *Free To Be Good or Bad* (see Appendix I). Dr. Holt observes that while analysis and counseling can be very valuable, you must remember that usually the analyst you go to will try to fit you into his own particular philosophy or approach to mental problems, his specific frame of reference, or his individual measure of psychological "modalities." In his book, Dr. Holt tells about a woman who had had a very happy marriage and had no ambitions other than being a good wife and homemaker. When her husband died, she recognized her need for guidance in getting through her grief. The analyst she chose happened to be a classic Freudian. After a few sessions Mrs. L. gave up on the therapy because, as she told a friend, "I know I'm screwed up, but one thing I know is not wrong with me is penis envy."

Turning a New Page

It's about this time, during the recoil period, when you realize that it's necessary to do something about your husband's possessions. Actually, this is a healthy decision, because cleaning is cleansing. When you know that you must bite the bullet and give away his clothes, empty out his wallet, and pack away or throw away his "souvenirs" (including his Marine Corps dogtags and his college term papers), you are well into the reality of your situation. You must go through this phase before you proceed to the next stages; not that they are necessarily better, but they are different.

Some widows can't face this housecleaning alone and must rely on friends and relatives to clean out closets. I was lucky in having a brother-in-law the same size as my husband who told me he "would be proud to wear Alex's clothes." A few days after the funeral my sister helped me pack them all up for her husband. Fortunately, they live in California, because I don't think I could bear seeing the same suits, shirts, and ties on a steady basis; but on my last visit, Gordon wore some of Alex's things and we all shared a few quiet tears and a few fond memories, and it was fine, okay.

In most cases, the best approach is to sort through possessions as quickly after the funeral as possible. Lorraine says, "The first time, the clothes stayed in the closet for a year and a half. And the prospect of giving them away didn't get any easier. I just couldn't, couldn't do anything. But the second time, I cleaned out Mike's things immediately—you see, I knew if I didn't, the job would still be ahead of me one or two years from then."

I disagree strongly with those who feel one must get rid of pipes, books, photographs, and other personal items that have actually made your home *your home*. After all, I never shove my children under the doormat when I'm meeting a new man, and they are the strongest reminder that another man has been there before him. By the same token, one shouldn't make a home a shrine to a dead husband . . . just as it shouldn't have been a *monument* to him when he was alive.

You'll find too that expedience does take over. The day you realize that empty closet in the bedroom can be very well used by you—that "Dad's bathroom" is really the private bathroom you've always coveted, that there's no point in saving his old prescriptions—that's the day you are beginning to emerge into what is at best, a brave new world.

Part 2

Re-entry: Back in the World

Widowhood is not like babyhood, when you can predict with a fair amount of certainty the first tooth, the first step, the first word. The lines between stages are fuzzy, dependent on so many factors they would snarl any computer seeking a pat set of statistics.

But at some point during or after the real grief time, slowly but surely you will begin to pick up your life again. And you will look around you and conclude it is indeed a *mess*. Your financial picture has changed, probably for the worse; if you have children, they are spinning in their own bewildered situation; what you thought was a solid social life has turned out to be an amorphous void, and your loneliness overwhelms you—it is more acute than ever. What to do?

Unfortunately, you can't deal with these problems one

at a time. You are engulfed by them and they all cry out for solution. Initially, unless you happen to be blessedly lucky or fantastically organized, you'll probably make a botch of most of the problems facing you . . . but slowly, slowly, some kind of sensible, or at least workable, picture will emerge. At the very least, you'll be able to say to yourself, "I'm functioning again."

This is not at all what our insurance researchers refer to as the "recovery" stage. Most widows I talked to concur with my own feelings that this is a special phase *before* recovery when you find yourself operating on four cylinders instead of eight. But at least you're moving.

For Ethel, who had to take over the operation of a farm when her husband died, friends and neighbors provided invaluable help. "They arrived almost immediately," to clean out the barns, sort out the machines for auction, cook dinners. She had to move more slowly, however, in assuming her new responsibilities. "It was like climbing stairs. You just take one step at a time."

Psychologist Roxanne Hiltz zeroes in on the problems of transition from one stage of widowhood to the next. First a widow must deal with the "grief work, the letting go of one's old emotional ties and roles which centered on the husband." Once this is accomplished, the second set of problems must be faced: "building a new life which provides financial security and a new social identity."

After Alex died, I buried myself in work for three months, not only because I had to earn money, but also because the work blunted, dulled the reality. I sat at my desk and wrote for ten or twelve hours a day, typing until one or two in the morning. The result was that I finished a book in record time, collected the rest of my advance, and blew it all on a trip to California and Mexico. It was only after I returned that I realized I had to start from scratch, or as much from scratch as one can with three children and the same house.

Barbara, the policeman's widow, also plunged into work. "I was in a state of shock. I went back to my job, but I'd just break down and cry. Or, I'd relive the whole thing, hoping it would come out differently, expecting my husband to come back." After six months she realized she had to get on with "the business of living. I owed it to my son."

Dr. Allan Fromme (Ph.D.), a New York psychologist, urges forward motion, taking action. "Nothing good will happen if you just sit around thinking, whereas when you act, things do get started. Some outcomes will be bad, but some will be good—it would be unreasonable to expect that after long periods of having tried *nothing*, every new activity will turn out to be splendidly worthwhile!"

According to Dr. Fromme, it is crucial to start slow. In his article, "Understanding Yourself Is Not Enough," in *Cosmopolitan* (May 1975), he wrote, "The more ambitious the undertaking, the smaller your first few steps should be . . . Small moves forward are possible, whereas big, sweeping changes often are not . . . Start easy—but keep moving. If you want a better social life, begin by making two luncheon dates, not by resolving to give a party for sixty sometime soon. Lonely? Arrange to spend one afternoon with your parents doing something they enjoy instead of prowling around bars every night looking for the grand amour.

"The point is once you start moving—getting out in the world and doing things—you'll start to change in subtle ways you won't even be aware of at first."

Inaction is described as "psychological hell," while action is definitely a healthy sign, so long as it represents *cautious* action. The following chapters will treat some of the ways you'll have to get moving during this interim stage . . . with some yellow blinkers to help prevent accidents.

4 | *The First-Year Crazies*

Soon after Alex died I received a phone call from a friend I hadn't seen since college who had heard the news via that invisible but effective old-friends-grapevine. A few years before, Tanya's husband had committed suicide, and she had known all the worst ramifications of widowhood, from the grievous shock of actually discovering the body to the horrendous entanglements and frustrations of no will, a hostile family, troubled children.

Tanya talked to me with the kind of understanding only one widow can have toward another, shared some of her "secrets" for survival, and gave me the soundest advice I had had until that point: Beware the First-Year Crazies!

She said, "Don't make any major changes in your life —none! Don't get married, don't sell the house, don't quit your column, don't do anything drastic until at least one year is over."

65

Her sensible advice kept me from moving to Mexico to marry the first romantic man who asked me. About the only major thing I did for one year was use some insurance money to tear out sliding glass doors and replace them with French doors, an architectural change I'd dreamed about for years—so that didn't count. (I did, however, manage some sticky *minor* crazies which I'll talk about later.)

But other widows, who didn't have the benefit of my friend's advice, have found themselves in various emotional and financial messes as a result of this peculiar but not atypical affliction—The First-Year Crazies, or what psychologists describe as "regressive or delinquent behavior."

One beautiful and rather well-known redhead who writes a newspaper column and has written several books on beauty and spas had been babied all through her married life by her husband who was twenty years her senior. When he died she found herself in an intolerable financial situation. This, coupled with loneliness and the neglect of her children (who, after all, played it tit-for-tat—she had always neglected them and left them to the care of nursemaids), propelled her into a disastrous marriage with a man she was too ready to believe was a good catch.

To save her from the horror of the chore, her new husband sent her to a spa while he efficiently sold all her previous domestic trappings—everything from pots, pans, sheets, towels, beds, appliances, and other homely but useful equipment, to her silver, china, antiques, and other prized possessions. With the promise of a fantastic new apartment, he moved her out of her eleven-room, rent-controlled penthouse and into a two-room suite at a New York hotel. And then he waited for her legacy to come through . . . and she waited for him to start spending all the money *she* thought *he* had. An O. Henry "Gift of the Magi" story in reverse.

She married him when her husband had been dead for eight months, divorced him five months later, and is now suing him for support money and the proceeds of her sold possessions, neither of which she has any chance of getting. (Conveniently, whatever assets he had were prenuptually turned over to his children). She now sublets a one-bedroom hotel apartment and has no hope of moving into her own place. (Think of the cost of replacing all those sheets, towels, sofas, beds). She literally doesn't have a pot . . . to boil tea in.

Another widow I talked to dealt with her temporary craziness by sleeping with a wide variety of men. This, incidentally, is incredibly easy to do because most men still believe that widows, like divorcees, are tremendously skittish and actually "hard up," (a wonderful, masculine term) and will be comforted and calmed by a little "loving." As a reward for her random sexual life, Gerry got a not-so-social disease at one point, had to have an abortion at another, and watched her more or less well-adjusted two young boys begin to stutter and have tantrums, a result of the barrage of "uncles" she subjected them to so soon after their father's death.

Gerry is not a normally promiscuous or even swinging lady. In fact, she had been happily and faithfully married for eleven years before her man died. The shock of it all drove her to some "crazy" solutions . . . until she discovered that sharing a bed with some brief encounter is no solution at all. Into her third year of widowhood, she's rebuilding her life with some solid direction.

For Alix, her crazies also involved "escape" by sleeping —alone—and she took to her bed for three months after her husband's death and would not answer calls, nor would she see friends. Now, two years later, she still refused to be interviewed and has not come to grips with the reality of her life.

She is an exception, however, because the majority of

the widows I interviewed did go on living in the "real" world, did take action, and did make mistakes. But they then moved on and are functioning in what may be a "patchy" existence, but is definitely one that is real.

Linda, who lives in Baltimore, turned to her church for comfort, in lieu of drugs or alcohol. "But the oddest thing was that although I went to church more often, I could never bear to stay around afterwards and talk to any of my friends. I would go to church and immediately leave."

Although she doesn't remember any really unusual actions during the first year of widowhood, she did refuse to visit her relatives, which led to family arguments. "I simply couldn't go to the same places I had been to with Ted. And even if friends asked me out to dinner, I refused to go. Maybe this was obstinate, even dumb, but you don't know where to turn because you've never been a widow before. You don't know what's going to make you happy or sadder."

After Marilyn emerged from her six months of numbness and many completed needlework projects, she remembers "going wild" for about a year and a half. "I was so frenetic—sexually, socially. I never stopped. And then after that time, I took another six months when I retreated and tried to decide what I wanted to do. That's really when I was able to function as a whole person, with good direction."

For Lisa and Nancy, a man was the way of acting out the crazies. Nancy began a long affair with a man six months after her husband died, and six months after that realized "I had made up this man. He wasn't at all what I thought he was, but I needed to have a direct relationship with someone. It took me another year before I was able to eject him from my life and begin living on my own."

Lisa describes her situation as a case of "getting very hungry to cook for a man. I started going out with a guy who in no way could ever be a permanent part of my life.

But I would go to great lengths to cook for him and enact the part of a wife. It was play-acting. I was playing house."

JoAnne played house in another way—she went back to her parents' home. "They were really supportive through Jack's illness, the funeral, everything. Then one weekend they said, 'Why don't you come over for dinner, bring the kids and stay overnight.' And I did, and this happened for Thanksgiving and Christmas and New Year's, but finally I realized I must stop this; I had to get back to my own life. I can't become dependent on them."

JoAnne also found that her parents were taking over *her* role as a parent and were disciplining the children, trying to reorganize their habits, criticizing how much or how little they ate. "It was as if my two boys and I suddenly became *their* three children, and of course they were after me for smoking and drinking, too."

Millie decided early on that she wouldn't sleep at a friend or relative's house. "I knew if I started that, I'd never be able to face sleeping in my own bed every night."

Getting to sleep at night was the problem that led to what Adelle recalls as her "crazies." She and her husband, Dan, used to talk out their days before falling asleep at night. "This was our special sharing time, and after he died I missed him most at bedtime, and also on Sundays. I missed the conversation and realized that not only was his voice absent, but at home I never heard *my* own voice anymore. So for several months I would talk into the tape recorder every night. Just as if Dan were here and we were having a normal conversation.

"Then the following night I would play back some of the tape so I could hear myself. I know it sounds kind of nutty, but it did act as a sort of diary, and little by little I stopped recording—maybe there would be gaps of four nights, then a week or so, and finally now, I don't talk into the tape. After eighteen months I'm used to a new routine and just read myself to sleep."

At first during our talk Suzanne couldn't recall anything especially "delinquent" in her behavior. "I was a
total wreck for at least nine months—tense, confused,
angry; I'm sure I made life miserable for Mark (her four-
year-old)." The mention of Mark seemed to spark her
memory and she realized that she, too, had had a run-in
with this first year malady. "About two months after
Stan died, Mark woke up one morning with a slight swelling over his eye. It looked like a rather aggravated mos-
quito bite. So I sent him off to nursery school. An hour
later they called me from the school—the swelling was really bad: it had grown to the size of a golf ball, and his
poor eye was almost lost by the swelling.

"I brought him home and put some ice on it and called
my pediatrician. He wouldn't be back at the office for two
more hours and the nurse suggested I take him to the
Holy Name emergency room. I packed him in the car,
started driving, and found I could not go to the hospital.
Stan had entered as an emergency-room patient, and of
course he died there. I could not make myself drive that
same route again. I turned around, drove home, and
sweated out the two more hours until I could see my doctor.

"Fortunately, it was a harmless spider bite—it looked
worse than it was—but afterwards I realized I was risking
Mark's life because of my own hang-up. What if he had
some terrible allergy to an insect? Those crazy deaths
from bee stings that you read about.

"A few weeks later I *made* myself drive to that emergency-room entrance; I had my cry, and I knew that if I
ever had to go there in the future, I could do it. But you
know, my next-door neighbor couldn't understand how I
could be so stupid, how I simply couldn't go there that
first time."

"A ridiculous drive toward self-improvement," is the

way Kate characterizes her first-year crazies. "I felt this need to learn new skills and over-extended myself with steno courses, tennis classes, cooking lessons, none of which I really had the heart to do. I filled in time with activities I wasn't ready for."

Paint was the form Alice's first year binges took. "About four months later I felt a need for movement, to be doing something in the hours when I couldn't work at writing. So I repainted the whole house, room by room, even though, with the exception of the laundry room, everything was pretty ship-shape. Ben and I used to enjoy doing the painting. We would open a few cans of beer, put our favorite records on the phonograph, and he would use the roller while I did all the trim.

"So for weeks I painted and painted. And cried and cried and cried. And listened to the old records. When it was finally over, I had a sparkling new house, but I really felt as if I had shed something. I had to get rid of this, maybe prove to myself it would be okay to do it alone. It was crazy, but the painting was definitely a catharsis."

Over-compensating, an urge to do too much, was my problem, too, but the worst ramifications occurred in a social sense when I was really guilty of over-kill. I found myself expounding at length and very pompously about world issues, or a new book, or even other people's personal problems in a way that bruised some long-standing friendships. The first time it happened I was very ashamed afterwards and could only chalk up the blame for my strident behavior on the fact that it was the week before my period—that old pre-menstrual tension. (Which was not entirely a cop-out.) The second and third times I took stands on subjects I believed in (a son boarding at college, and a wife going to work for the first time), but which were not worth getting into near armed-warfare about. Politely, socially, as a friend, I should have soft-pedalled my very opinionated remarks.

Looking back on it now, I think I was trying to assert myself—*me*—trying to prove that without Alex I was still a person with some worthwhile opinions and information. But I was more than a few degrees off-target. It wasn't necessary to be an argumentative, social boor to establish my own identity. Having recognized this, I've calmed down somewhat since then . . . but I still do enjoy pricking a few holes in overstuffed egos and saying quasi-outrageous things at parties so that people won't wrap me up and tag me as a "Poor soul—widow."

The poor soul is just the image some widows adopt as a result of their first-year adjustments. Although very few women in our country, of our generation, wear mourning for any length of time, a good many widows wear a different type of mourning. They choose their oldest, sloppiest, least presentable clothes to face the world. And, predictably, the world turns away. It's crazy to look like a wreck when you go to the market, to your children's school conferences, or to work. It's healthy to clean out your closets and get rid of the oldies and baddies. No matter how tight your budget, squeeze some funds out of it for one or two good-looking new things. Your head will feel better if you look better, and in addition, you never know when you might bump into someone special at the supermarket.

The first-year crazies can affect anyone. Even best-selling author Lynn Caine made a drastic move from the life she had known as an apartment dweller in New York City, to the misguided choice of living in a New Jersey suburb, where in addition to her personal problems, she was faced with the unfamiliar adventure of running a house. This is fraught with everyday frustrations any homeowner knows, from the lawn acquiring some unknown fungus to the plumbing conking out at the most inconvenient times. Her move was costly, debilitating, and lesson-teaching.

For some widows, the solution to avoiding dumb decisions and actions is readily at hand, and it lies in carrying through on a set routine. Eve says, "I went back to my place of business the day after the funeral. I made a point of spending time after work with several of my employees who were also single. And I played a lot of golf. I made my life so busy there was no room to reflect on my grief."

Karen, who doesn't work full-time but has always been involved with volunteer activities, the local school board, and tennis, explains that she "plunged" right back into her normal schedule. "I was lucky enough to have good friends, too, who asked me away for weekends or out to dinner." The one situation which Karen feels she has not mastered is that she can no longer read a book—after more than two years of widowhood. "I can't explain this, I can't understand it. I can read the newspapers or a short magazine article, but I can't handle a book."

For Helen, what seemed like a crazy solution—taking over part of her husband's counseling practice with limited experience—actually turned out to be solid therapy for her as well as her clients. "This decision helped me professionally and emotionally. Yet looking back on it, it was a formidable action to take."

Marilyn found herself "returning to the womb," even though her social life had some antic aspects to it. "After Paul died, I sold our house in Palm Springs—everything included, furniture, sheets, the whole works—and I took what little money was left and bought myself a small co-op in New York. This made me feel secure, it was a start." Looking back on the ten years since she's been a widow, she says, "When Paul died, I thought, 'I'm just going to change my personality, become a whole different person' . . . not realizing that the experience had already made me a totally different person. Now I feel I'm me; I tell people how old I am; and I'm always honest. I have a very definite need to be natural and honest."

A booklet published by the American Association of Retired Persons and the National Retired Teachers Association, while slanted for older widows, has some very good practical advice. In "Your Retirement Widowhood Guide," the writer refers to a condition known as "I-ness," and recommends that you avoid the first-year crazies by not jumping into changes in living and status that your I-ness doesn't endorse wholeheartedly. "Don't let yourself become hemmed in" represents the thrust of the message. Put your "I into action, to join it up with the rest of your body." Be able to say, "I just have to do what's right for me, so I can get my life going again."

Sometimes in the confusion and grief, one loses sight of that "I-ness" in the long, first year after a husband dies. If you seem to be faltering, or are questioning what may be a bad choice, keep in mind my sensible friend Tanya's advice about not making drastic decisions. Another good watchword to live by was passed on by my father, who told me, in Italian, *"Chi va piano, va sano e va lontano."* He who goes slowly goes safely and goes a long way.

5 | *The Children*

Coping with children under sound, sensible, "happily married" circumstances can be an unending challenge at best and a discouraging, frustrating failure at worst. Witness recent books that far outclass Dr. Spock in scope, including *P.E.T.—"Parent Effectiveness Training"* and *Dare to Discipline* (see Appendix III).

But the children of one-parent homes are even more of a handful. According to the last government census, one out of every six children under eighteen years old today is living in a single-parent family (almost double the figures of 1950), and in 1975, there were 7.2 million households headed by women playing both father and mother to 10.5 million kids. In some ways the difficulties of divorced-parent children are similar to those of widowed-parent children, but in other ways they are quite different.

In so many cases, children of divorce are either torn between the two parents or much too attached to one of them, a situation that sets up conflicts and jealousy; but at least there is the real presence of a father to take some of the pressure off the mother—even on a part-time basis. The child whose father is dead must face not only the ultimate, scary finality of the death of someone he loved and enduring grief, but he must also hobble along in that "different" way no child likes. When I was a little girl I hated wearing braces; today, if you don't wear braces, you're "different." But today if you don't have a father or mother, you're different, and the effect is that children feel ashamed as well as bereft: something is wrong with them personally.

In *On Being Alone* (see Appendix I), Dr. James A. Peterson writes, "We do not do well with the fact of death in our society. Children are often the victims of having been so shielded from any exposure to death that they are terror-stricken when death occurs . . . They have nightmares and day terrors. They worry about the living parent and their own future."

Kate was told that her fifteen-year-old brain-damaged daughter "has not reconciled her father's death. She fantasizes a great deal and I'm not sure what is going on in her head. But I do know that she is terrified about being left alone, that something will happen to me."

As Joyce Brothers points out, "The widow is so involved in her own grief that often she can't help her children. And children don't verbalize the fact that they are bereft. They use withdrawal as a way of protecting themselves. We should encourage children to talk out their grief."

Joyce Phipps, founder of New Haven's Outreach program, remembers that after her husband died of a heart attack, her six-year-old son wouldn't talk about it. "Weeks went by and not a word; then I guess I'd given him one spanking too many. He screamed at me: 'I wish you were dead. I want my daddy.' "

Marian's children were three- and four-years-old when their father died. "I knew I had to make them understand it was nothing they did that made their daddy die." As Helen points out, "For a child, when somebody dies it's a rejection, a form of abandonment."

In addition, the mother's situation with her children changes markedly, too.

When your children are over 15 or 16, you may be able to share your grief and work it out together; but if your kids are under that age, you are going to be faced with a separate set of reactions for each child.

My case, with my children aged 10, 7, and 3 when Alex died, required coping with individual variations of grief, including my own. Maria, then 10, stopped believing in God and still balks at going to Sunday School—her God has betrayed her. Sandy, whose seventh birthday occurred on the day I was told there was no possible chance for Alex to live, was too quiet about his loss and for a long time insisted on talking about his father in the present tense. For months he reverted to babyish habits and would burst into tears too readily when frustrated. Robbie, then 3, initially thought Dad was in heaven and/or the hospital with God and the doctors; now he knows Dad's in the cemetery with his own tombstone. He asks me if Dad eats down there, or if he has to go to the bathroom, and is confused about whether Dad is really "down" (in the ground) or "up" in heaven. Recently he brought me a small, square rock and said, "This is a tombstone for babies; Dadas have bigger ones."

Robbie also went through a time of asking every repairman, garbageman, train conductor, salesman, any man whom he responded to (and he responds to most men), if they would be his daddy. One progresses, though, in grief and widowhood, and at first I cried; but eventually, I began to smile and then laugh at this very enterprising little boy in need of a father. (He is currently saving his five-pennies-a-week allowance because he wants me to *buy* a father, and I told him that new fathers were about as expensive as a new car. Actually, he's torn between saving for a car and saving for a father.)

Jill had much the same experience. "Essentially, Billy had never had a father, and it is almost impossible to find male-oriented activities for a boy under six. He gleaned what he could from my male friends. Even now, when he's almost seven, he inquires of every date I have, 'Are you going to be my Daddy?' "

As Dr. Spock wrote in the article "A Father's Companionship," in *Redbook* (October 1974), "Children deprived of a father . . . will always try to fill the gap by idealizing the friendly men in their lives—grandfathers, uncles, teachers, tradesmen, men their mother dates, or the man she may marry. In other words, children know that they need a father-figure and will create one out of whatever materials are at hand."

Beth went so far in search of a father-figure that she prolonged her first relationship with this in mind. "He was an excellent father substitute and I was honest with him. The kids adored him. But after it ended, I decided no more. I preferred to be alone, or felt I must face being alone and being a single parent."

The problems relating to children under these circumstances are myriad and vary according to the ages, numbers, and personal psyches of the kids, in combination with the mental state of the mother. Rita's children, for example, who had been brought up in a very father-oriented Armenian household, rebelled when their father died. In a sense they had lost their "rudder," and Rita, who had always been the competent but retiring mother in the background, wasn't able to cope with the adolescence of these non-directed kids. They loved their mother, but they became small-time revolutionaries—disobeying her curfews, neglecting chores, getting into trouble at school. Although she tried to adopt the strong hand of their father, there was no way they could accept her in *his* role. "I could see them slipping from me, see that my authority was a joke, but I couldn't do a thing except go on cooking their meals and taking care of their clothes. I'm just hoping they'll get through this all right and straighten out. Even my priest can't tell me what to do."

In some cases, older children take on the role of "the father" and are supportive to the other children as well as to the widow. When Virginia's husband died, her nineteen-year-old son from her first marriage held the family together and gave his seven-year-old half-sister and four-year-old half-brother the kind of love and care needed to get through the first bad months. Virginia said, "Jack was a rock for all of us. A few years later he told me this was a turning point in his life. That he had grown up that summer. In his case it was a good thing for him to be able to take that responsibility."

Another nineteen-year-old, David, however, couldn't believe that his father was dead, even though he knew he had been terminally ill. His mother, Anita, says, "When I called him at school to tell him, he couldn't accept it. He had completely shut out the possibility that this could happen. One of the long-lasting results of Frank's death, and this was reinforced when his grandmother died, is that David has absolutely no faith in doctors. He doesn't believe them, doesn't trust them, doesn't think they do what they should be doing."

Sarah's fifteen- and thirteen-year-old boys never discussed their father's death. "Although we talk about my husband often, they never ask questions about death or why he died. Recently, though, my older son wrote a story for school about a grandfather who lived in the house and died of cancer, and I think this was Steven's way of verbalizing Hal's death."

Dr. Peterson notes that "adolescent children may be even more of a problem because they are trying to achieve independence but have not quite made it. They tend to over-react: either collapse in grief or not want to talk at all. But this will pass, and eventually they will be able to react 'normally.' "

Jamie, Nanette Fabray's eighteen-year-old son, is very protective of his mother and wants to take care of her, but he's also torn because he wants to be with his friends. Nanette found it difficult to be both father and mother, especially since her work takes her away for part of the year and her son can only travel with her some of the time. "But now that he's going to college, it will be a real break from home and me," which Nanette feels he urgently needs.

The lack of a father-figure is crucial in all these instances, from the normal father/child activities such as throwing a football, reading a report card, or helping with math homework. The snags are compounded according to the extent to which your husband played his role as father. If *you* were always the disciplinarian, this will not be too much of a change; but if your kids were used to a balance of discipline and fun from two different parents, and it now comes down hard from just one, watch out—trouble ahead.

You can counter it by bringing in some heavy father-substitutes . . . but even these don't work because most males—fathers, brothers, uncles, friends—are going to be *kind* to these fatherless kids and let them get away with murder.

Personally, I decided to hire a young man who could work with the kids, but would be adept enough to provide some discipline and direction as well. Instead of relying on sitters last summer, I felt the kids had had enough "female" influence in their lives, and I searched for a young man who could spar with them, swim with them, show them how to play tennis, and administer a good verbal or actual spank when required. I was fortunate, really lucky, to find John through a collegiate "house-sitting" service; he's a college student who loves kids, has a marvelous sense of understanding and a good approach to discipline, and, incidentally, was of practical and therapeutic help to *me* too. He cut the hedges, cleaned the swimming pool, and talked to me about my problems in dealing with the kids as well.

Mostly though, whether you are lucky enough to find your own John, or whether your father can sub for your kids' father, usually you will have to act as father *and* mother, a self-defeating horror. About the only real goody in the pile is the element of love; your children will grow closer to you with a very intuitive sense of knowing you need them and they need you, and that's great.

Beth remembers, "Looking back, the experience was a good one in a crazy sense. I asked for their support and got it. They did cling to me a lot but that passed with maturity. At times they seemed a burden (still do), but I was thankful for their existence."

Mutual need was reiterated by Irene: "Although Randy was too young to understand, Cleo was able to comprehend fully and was miserably upset. And there were times I could not hide my despair from her, and she comforted and consoled me in some primal way that no adult could. I constantly reinforced the fact that Daddy loved them very much. This helped. Cleo had fits of crying but made fast recovery. During the next few years, of course, the single-parent position created its own problems."

Another fact you'll have to cope with is that although you love them deeply, children are basically selfish little animals—they have to be to survive. They are more resilient and more demanding; they will learn to take advantage of you; and you may be all too ready to *let* them take advantage because of guilt, fatigue, or any number of reasons. The going is going to be rough.

This is characteristic of a nationwide parental hang-up, not just indigenous to a widow's woes. Says Dr. Spock, "Americans don't love their children more or make greater sacrifices for them than parents in other parts of the world. But they *worry* more about whether they are doing the right thing for them and about whether their children love them."

When Ethel was widowed at 30, with two children under 8, although she considered walking away from the farm and its responsibilities, ultimately she felt, "Whatever I did, it had to include what was best for our children. It would be what Tom wanted."

It's not uncommon to think that anything that goes wrong with the children is your fault, because they don't have a father and you're not doing a good job. I went through one period of over-compensating—with love, vacations, material goodies, and "trade-offs." I would let them stay up longer than they should because they were so "good," or I would be too harsh with them if they were bad. I knew this was erratic, but I couldn't seem to find the right balance.

Then, at one point a few months ago, all three of the children's teachers called me, requesting personal conferences. Maria wasn't doing as well in school as she should have been; Sandy was daydreaming and not turning in his assignments; and my gentle Robbie was fighting with other children. After the meetings it was clear that Maria was opting for a sixth-grade social life instead of being the class "brain"; Sandy was just plain bored with reading (a situation that changed when he was given a new reading book); and Rob was ready for spring vacation and nervous because I was nervous about finishing this book.

After these three summit meetings, I had a good long talk with myself and decided that the situation wouldn't have been very different had Alex been alive . . . that these were problems "normal" two-parented kids had and I shouldn't feel so guilty about "failing."

Guilt plagued Maureen, too: "I craved eating alone and being alone. The children were demanding and I wanted peace. Our life didn't change that much, except now the kids were with me constantly, going everywhere. I felt guilty leaving them. I felt I should be around most of the time and that they needed me. I was overwhelmed by the sense of responsibility, and it was only after a year that I was able to get out and take some art classes."

Another problem is that when you're down, the kids are too, and everybody behaves badly. There will have to be some times when you all break down and cry. There will also have to be times when you do say, biting your tongue all the while, "Your father would really whack you for that," or, "You wouldn't do that if Dad were here." They might or they might not have done that if Dad were here. Now that you're alone, where is it written that you must be Super-Parent? Although you can't protect them from what is, after all, their reality too, you should be allowed some mistakes . . . just try not to take out your emotional problems on them. And as Janet pointed out, even though you may try at times to be a super-parent to compensate for their father's absence, "ironically, because of all the problems, you often are less of a parent now than you were to begin with."

Kate says, "I tried to be very strong, but now I know I should have shared my grief with my child, instead of being stoic. It would have helped to let her know how troubled I was (and am) at times. But I've only come to this knowledge very recently, and I still find it difficult to act like a total, complete family."

Dr. T. Berry Brazelton, author of *Toddlers and Parents*

(see Appendix III), tells about Mrs. B., a widow who was left with a young child. "She sees every slight mis-step in Tony's behavior as evidence that she is a bad mother and he a damaged child. Learning that other mothers have the same problems with their children should be a real bulwark against these feelings."

Another problem is the assigning of new roles to the children . . . or their own assumption of roles that they aren't really old enough to handle. I remember that on Thanksgiving, the first major holiday after Alex died, a relative suggested that Sandy, then 7, sit at his father's place at the head of the table, since he was "the man of the house now." Sandy was *not* the man of the house. He was a seven-year-old who had lost his father. We quickly decided my *father* should take that honored, but responsible place instead—until the time Sandy felt comfortable about claiming it. This past Easter, a year and a half after Alex's death, I routinely placed my Dad at the head of the table, and just before dinner Sandy asked, rather timidly, if he could please sit there instead!

As another example, Maria has become very motherly. She frets over my not eating enough and smoking too much, and tries to bolster up my confidence by telling me how nice I look. She even checks up on me every night while I'm working to see how it's going. "Are you on a hot streak?" she'll ask, and grin if I tell her it's moving well. When I'm blocked for the moment, she offers to make me a cup of tea, fix me a sandwich, or will very practically inform me I've worked long enough and should come watch "Maude" with her.

But then, practicality, along with self-preservation, is another common trait of children. They know, very sensibly, that they *need* another father. While Robbie saves his pennies, Maria, now 12, almost wistfully says to me whenever I'm going out on a date, "Maybe you'll meet someone nice," and last night when Sandy saw a particularly bright star around the moon, and knew from his "Star Trek" viewings this could well be a supernova, but also *might* just be a special star, he made a wish that "I could get him a new daddy."

While some children wish for a new daddy, others see any new man as a rival for the *old* daddy's position, and according to widows I talked to, daughters around the age of nine or ten are fiercely loyal to their fathers. Joan had a boyfriend visit her beach house, along with two or three other couples. Although her younger son adores Jack, Amy (10) was furious when she saw his suitcase in her mother's room. "She wouldn't speak to me for hours, but wanted me to guess what was wrong. I knew she was angry because she realized I was having sex with Jack, but I sat her down and explained what daddy would have wanted for me.

"The point is she was being very manipulative. Her life is fine, she's involved, but she doesn't want me to have any kind of freedom, especially if it involves her feelings about her father. It was necessary for me to tell her strongly that she couldn't dictate to me and run my life."

Even a toddler can try to exercise control over his single parent. Dr. Brazelton reports that Tony, who never knew his father, would create confusion whenever his mother was on the phone and therefore not paying strict attention to him. "Once, when a male friend came by to take her out, Tony went wild. He showed off painfully, was coy with the man, and teased his mother mercilessly. When she started to leave Tony with the sitter, he had what seemed to be an endless tantrum."

Well, my children, who are older, have their variations on the same theme. And I never know if this sudden epidemic of bad behavior stems from their fear because I'm leaving, if they are sad because a man other than their Dad is paying attention to me, or if they are simply jealous because they want to star in the show themselves. Although they want me to have fun, a real dichotomy exists in their actions when someone wants to take me out—whether it's a "date" or simply an old friend.

Widows with older children who have left home and are on their own, perhaps married and raising their own families, have an entirely different set of problems and reactions. My talks with women in these circumstances indicate that it's difficult to steer a straight course and retain their own identity without becoming burdens or "obligations." "I don't want my kids to see me just because I need them or I'm lonely," said Amy, independently. "Sometimes I think my kids couldn't care less, or that they put up with me because of my problems," said Mary, somewhat bitterly. In truth, most mothers, not just widows, feel their grown-up children don't call enough or do enough. So much depends on how the family group was structured to begin with, whether it was close-knit or everyone was on his own. If your family fell into the latter category, it is impractical and unrealistic now to expect that your children will suddenly fill the void left by your husband's death.

Unanimously, widowed mothers agree that among the hardest times are those when the children do something that their fathers would have been proud of. The women mentioned major and minor events in life, from hitting a home run, a daughter's first date, to graduation from college or getting married. "I started to cry, because my husband should have seen this."

It helps to give the children something that belonged to their father to make them feel included and important and to carry on his memory in a positive way. I gave Sandy Alex's digital clock and Robbie his brass shoe horn and wallet; Maria got his FM radio and his hockey puck, which she sleeps with under her pillow every night. As I unearth other things—books, a magnifying glass, a favorite ruler—I dole them out. Alex was a painter as well as a writer, so I went through his canvases and had the children pick out their favorites, which we hung in their rooms. Go through photographs; sort out the diplomas and other souvenirs. This is an important transition stage that helps your children realize that although their father is gone, they have a special part of him all their own to be proud of and remember him by.

Dr. Brazelton says, "Being an only parent is lonely work. There's no one else to pick up the pieces at the end of the day, no one to start baths or turn them off, no one to answer the telephone while you are (busy with the children) . . . and, most important of all, no one but children to talk to."

In your own road back to life, you're going to have to deal with a lot of "givens," and one of them, for you and the children, is to accept the fact that there is no actual father in the house. Although algebra equations with givens always have a solution, right now you're stuck with the givens and *no* solution. You have a new set of circumstances to deal with that are just as real as the "given" of having a father around—but no simple "home-again-at-six-o'clock" answer is in sight.

The major point is that your children are going through their own "impact-recoil-recovery" period too . . . and the path to the last stage is paved with trauma.

6 | *It's Only Money*

"Money, money, money, money, money, money, money." Joel Grey and Liza Minelli satirized the concept of money so beautifully in *Cabaret*. But money is hardly a subject of satire with widows—too often it becomes an overriding interest based on some very disparate but demanding realities.

You need money to take care of your family; you may never have managed the family finances before; you may already be working in a job to provide that money, but need a better job to provide more money and/or provide some personal social benefits for you; you may not be able to *find* a job because you've never worked before or haven't worked for years; you may constantly be short of money (which means you're not only perennially broke but have to face the sticky bit of telling your kids or yourself "we can't afford this"). Money, money, money. The

89

ramifications are mind-bending; the answers not readily apparent.

A booklet published by Anchor National Financial Services of Phoenix to prepare wives for the eventuality of widowhood, details some of the cold, hard facts:

● On an average, a family's income after a husband's death is reduced by 44 percent, including all Social Security and pension benefits and the working income of the widow who *already* has a job. In families with previous incomes of $15,000 or more, the decrease jumps to a 57 percent change!

● 52 percent of widows queried had used up all their life insurance benefits within eighteen months; 25 percent ran through such benefits within *two months.*

● Of the 56 percent of widows who were working two years after their husbands' deaths, 93 percent reported needing the income, but two-thirds would work even if there were no financial need. (Of those who would stop working if they had a financial windfall, 42 percent were mothers of preschoolers.)

● At the age of 35, widowed, divorced, or separated women can expect to work another twenty-eight years (just six months less than the work-life prediction for a man of 35).

Not in the sense of "misery loves company," but rather in the spirit of "there's strength in numbers," some of the ways other women have dealt with their "filthy lucre" flaps will be discussed.

Budgets

People are always telling you how necessary it is to have a budget. Two things come to mind. Budgets are fine if you have enough money to stick into each little envelope; then, too, some women function better by looking at the total picture instead of apportioning so much for rent, so much for entertainment, etc.

Still, the traditional view is the one put forth by financial authorities and estate managers, and it amounts to a system of either literal or figurative little envelopes. To plan a budget, you first add up your assets—the money in checking accounts and savings accounts, a car, home, any other personal property and the current value of investments. Secondly, you figure out your debits—what you owe on loans, mortgages, charge accounts, and other debts. By subtracting liabilities from assets you know what your net worth is.

But that's just the start: now you have to figure out how to manage your money. You can do this in six steps, according to a well-written but overly optimistic booklet, Let's Talk About Money (see Appendix IV), published by The American Council of Life Insurance.

> **1.** *Add up your total income.* If you work, use your take-home pay as the amount. Add Social Security, interest from savings, dividends from life insurance or stock.
>
> **2.** *Account for your total fixed expenses.* Taxes, mortgage, car payments, church, telephone, utilities.
>
> **3.** *Determine day-to-day living expenses.* Food, clothing, transportation, entertainment, children's allowances, home or car repairs. (I always add another $100 a month to this "wish-list" for miscellaneous contingencies).
>
> **4.** *Decide what you need for savings.*
>
> **5.** *If there's any money left over, decide how you might use it to increase your assets.*
>
> **6.** *If there isn't any money left over, go over your spending plan again. Can you reduce some of your day-to-day items? Take a really close look at your "fixed" costs.*

The booklet is pleasant, straightforward, and somewhat

helpful, but clearly the writers have a rather sophomoric understanding of the financial problems most widows face. Of all the women I talked to, perhaps 5 percent had no money worries and could work out such a sensible six-step program. And of that percentage, half were constantly worried that something might go wrong and that they would have to dip into savings or capital. Nancy, who frankly admits she's making more money now as an editor than she ever did in her life, says she feels "sick" when she has to borrow $500 against her insurance to cover unexpected but continually occurring bills such as orthodontia for her son or the replacement of a sofa that has "absolutely collapsed."

Obviously, no person on a fixed income can spend helter-skelter—and just as obviously, if you have no money problems at all, you can skip a few paragraphs here. But most widows are always broke, and the problem is not so much budgeting as *juggling.*

"I'm constantly robbing Peter to pay Paul," says one widow. "But it always works out more or less okay and I find myself about fifty bucks down every month." She laughs when I mention savings. "There simply isn't room for any. I make sure I take care of all my insurance policies first—health, homeowner's, car. When I take a vacation, I do it on an extended payment plan so I have twelve months to pay instead of all at once. There is no possible way I can set aside a certain amount every month, even for the children's education; I feel it's more important to do things with them now."

Although it may sound like an irresponsible fiscal policy, JoAnne has a very pragmatic sense of direction: "An insurance agent tried to convince me that I needed life insurance with my kids as beneficiaries. I would pay about $60.00 a month and at age 65, if I were still alive, I'd receive around $20,000. If I died before that, my three kids would split $25,000, or about enough to send each of them to college for one or two years. First of all, the odds against my dying are in my favor—I'm forty-one. More to the point, I own a house worth $75,000; if I were to die prematurely, after the mortgage is paid $60,000 would go to my children—the best bequest I could leave them. In the meantime, I'm spending that $60.00 a month paying for the trip to Guadeloupe we took last year, and next year I plan to spend that amount on a trip to either the Caribbean or Spain. One thing my husband's death taught me was to live for the moment—and I intend to have as many good moments for myself and with my kids that I can."

I find myself pretty much in JoAnne's boat—a house with a reasonable enough mortgage, a fixed amount of Social Security ($570 a month), a small V.A. pension, and the rest of my income determined by how much I earn through writing, which definitely does not guarantee a steady income. The only way I can take a vacation, buy a car (and I haven't been able to accomplish this yet, despite Robbie's savings), or make any major repairs on the house is to do it via the installment plan, with the help of my friendly local bank.

Yet even aside from these major budget-breakers, there is never enough to cover the necessities. In lieu of the old-fashioned envelopes with cash in them, at the beginning of every month I write out checks for all the bills I would like to pay, or have to pay, and stuff them in their respective envelopes. Then I project the money that is *actually* coming in, optimistically include the earnings that are due . . . and endure that once-a-month depression when I see, quite simply, that the balance sheet won't balance. The situation becomes worse when a promised check never arrives.

Occasionally I use Sandy's calculator, but even with mechanical assistance, I am still short after long hours of bookkeeping. Short! That word was used by the widows I interviewed about as frequently as they used *shock* to describe their reactions when their husbands died.

Although the truth of the figures cannot be denied, I can't live in a crabbed, desperate way, always knowing I can't afford something and stoically doing without. If I don't have the house painted, it depresses me; the peeling paint is an indication to me that I'm not making it. So I have the house painted and I feel better—even though it means shuffling some of those already-written checks into next month's pile, on the hope, again, that some of those promised funds will come in.

I should not take a vacation each year in February, but if I don't, I'll die a little inside. I need to feel that for two or three weeks, my life is in order, I am having nothing but a good time with my children, and most of all, I'm gathering strength for the next twelve-month interim with its social, financial, and emotional ups and downs.

A good month is when I'm short only $100 or so; a bad month is the one when I need four new tires for the car or the toilet breaks and floods into the den ceiling, which has to be replaced at a cost of $490. When this happens, I try to extend my line of credit at the bank, and if I can't, I put some more checks aside to pay maybe *next* month, and then steel myself to the wave of pink, green, blue, yellow, angry "friendly reminders" that my account is past due. Last month the air conditioner broke down ($79.00), the car battery conked out (in the cemetery, of all places—$42.00), and the T.V. set refused to work unless it had four new "minor" tubes ($36.00). I knew that if one more thing broke down, *I* would break down!

Obviously the concept of a nest-egg or "cushion" is as far-fetched for me as it is for JoAnne.

"Short," was the conclusion of Kate, whose total yearly income is $13,000—$2,000 from Social Security, the rest from her job at an Illinois library. "Coming from a simple home I learned to spend money on first priorities: a roof over my head and food on the table. I'm short every month for anything other than basics."

"Short," said Aunt Rose, who has had over thirty years of dealing with deficits. "In the early days of Social Security, I only received $24.00 a month and couldn't earn more than $14.40, or I would lose my benefits. Even in the depression you couldn't live on that!" Aunt Rose babysat and for a year or so became a live-in housekeeper— for cash—to get around the government limits. Today, at 65, she's retired and gets full Social Security and some help from Medicare. And guess what: "I'm still short every month."

Although Peter had life insurance, Irene's family income was reduced by 50 percent after he died. She invested her capital in bonds, but the interest and Social Security are not quite enough. She lives on about $14,000 a year, "and I get through each month with a little help from my credit cards."

Peggy is as strapped as most of us for monthly cash, but despite other needs, she finds it reassuring to deposit her husband's $90.00 veteran's pension into savings accounts for her three children. "I've missed a few months since he died a year ago, when some kind of money emergency came up, but basically I find that while $90.00 a month doesn't really solve my day-to-day financial problems, it makes me feel good to know that by banking it, I'm doing something for their future."

Gloria, an executive secretary in her forties, does live according to a budget, although her late husband earned a substantial amount. "Jeff was the kind of man who couldn't get to the bank. When he received a check for a business deal he'd come home with a car or a house, or a trip planned. It was fun, but even then I was much more conservative. Now, of course, I have to be, because when he died his income died, too, but I manage to do enough of the things I want to do and live the way I like through my own earnings."

Recently there has been some attention on the part of major insurance companies and other financial advisors to the need for a wife to handle family finances, or at least participate in budgeting and planning while her husband is still alive. In several booklets, for example, Anchor National Financial Services of Phoenix have pointed out that this preventive measure will make a wife a better and more knowledgeable financial manager when she is a widow.

Jobs: Getting One

As *Time* magazine reported in a special issue (March 20, 1972) on women, "Today when they (women) try to enter the labor market at mid-life after a decade or two of absence—or after never having worked at all—they find that employers consider them qualified for only the lowest jobs. The skills and knowledge that they acquired in college or in a few years of work before marriage have become obsolete. Among college educated women, the problem is particularly difficult for female liberal arts graduates (sometimes knows as FLAGS), who often have little in the way of easily marketable skills. After years of confident supremacy in the kitchen, they find themselves in a new and often hostile world, like a nun who has recently left the convent."

"What are your skills? What is your training? What can you do *professionally*?" Well, you majored in art history, raised three children, were president of the P.T.A., and worked on negotiations for teacher contracts. With this record you certainly couldn't get a job as an Art Director in an ad agency, but you could swing a position as a receptionist-assistant at a museum. This was the case with the mother of a college roommate who managed to wrap up the positive aspects of her twenty years as a housewife and landed an onward and upward post as an administrative assistant at New York's Museum of Modern Art.

In looking for a job, it's not necessary to think in standard career terms, especially if you're free from the responsibility of caring for young children. One widow, Inga E. Angel, is a professional croupier who earns her money dealing baccarat and Joker-7 (a game similar to roulette) aboard cruise ships. Inga took the job as "therapy" after her husband died in 1973. She had no training for this career whatsoever, but after a crash course at a special school in Las Vegas, she now teaches other women to deal. She doesn't see this as a long-range solution, but it did get her through the first awful times, both mentally and financially, and she's still enjoying her unusual career.

Another widow who lacked special training is Ruth, who had worked as her husband's Girl Friday but then left his machine shop to raise a family. When her husband died, she was forced to take over the company—this was her major asset and source of financial support—although she knew nothing about management, much less machines. "But it seemed as if God spoke to me and said, 'I will be with you and give you the words.' " She talked to the people at the shop and they all agreed to stay with her and help. She had to make dozens of financial decisions, determine the market value of equipment she wasn't using, and watch out for people ready to take advantage of her.

"As the months passed, I felt I was becoming more perceptive, more controlled . . . But was I really making it? We were still running awfully close to that thin red line." She turned to God again and seemed to get some answers—she was holding on. One year after Ernie's death, she had a session with her accountant: "the moment of truth." The business was functioning profitably and she had the confidence of her customers. She attributes it all to "The Boss around here—God."

Aunt Rose also had no special training but found she had two other strikes against her as well: "I couldn't drive a car which made it difficult to get to a job, and I was over forty, and in those days that was a handicap." Despite these drawbacks, she started from scratch as a bank clerk and later became a teller with some special responsibilities. The fact that she worked into this job and stayed with it for over ten years ultimately enabled her to collect her full Social Security benefits—skimpy as they are.

Of all women in the United States today, 43 percent work, amounting to over 38 percent of the nation's total labor force. The situation is better than it was twenty years ago for Aunt Rose . . . but not that much easier to crack. Today, a woman over 40 is regarded with more respect because usually she will not have young children who get sick (which would mean days off the job); if she's a widow she will not be getting pregnant and therefore leaving after a few months. But the competition is still there—from women the same age who perhaps have had better training, or from those who have supportive husbands and therefore don't need as much money.

If you're over 50, employers are not worrying about pregnancy, but they are worrying about your health and how long you are willing to stay on the job before retiring. Dorothy Kostka, writing in *The Denver Post* about job opportunities for "mature" women, said, "If I were over fifty, widowed, and looking for a job, I would tint that white hair whatever color it used to be. I would reduce my age to fifty or over forty. It is annoying to be forced to cater to our youth culture, but this is a question of survival. If I were too plump, I would knock off some pounds and shape up. I would freshen up my wardrobe and buy a new outfit for job applying, if I needed it. The trifocals and the dentures must stay, but many people younger than fifty are sporting these."

If you need a job urgently, for whatever reason, it may be better to sidestep the positions you would love but are hard to land because they require more experience than you have. Instead, pay attention to jobs with possibilities for the future in terms of your own interests and financial needs. It might be worth it to take a so-so job now while you brush up on the qualifications for another step up the ladder. This has been said so many times, but it's worth repeating once more: typing is a very good way of getting your foot in the door. With natural aptitude and talent, in a few months you could well be out of the typists' pool and into the executive swim.

Another good door-opener is a knack for selling. Virginia has an instinctive clothes sense and a talent for talking to people. She talked herself into a job as a sales clerk at a chain of boutiques. Within six months her boss was taking her along on buying trips now and then because Virginia seemed to know intuitively what would "move" and what wouldn't. A few weeks ago she called me to say she had been promoted to Assistant Manager of her store, was taking courses in merchandising and buying, and had been promised a job as a full-fledged manager (with some buying responsibilities) at the very next opening.

If you're confused or dispirited about what kind of job you could find, or how to "merchandise" your own abilities, there are many free or very inexpensive job counseling services available through such unrelated sources as community colleges, local churches, YWCAs, even some altruistic major companies. In my own town, for example, a major publishing house provides counseling and is very encouraging about hiring local women—to the point that they give mothers school holidays off. Their 8:30 to 4:30

hours make it convenient for working mothers to get on the job and get home early enough to care for and cook dinner for young families. (One friend has a first-grader and has been able to find a teenager who is delighted to earn $10.00 a week by babysitting for a few hours every day.)

Other sources for job counseling—and getting—are listed in Appendix V. But basically, the major thrust is up to you. Read the classified ads assiduously, take the plunge and go on job interviews (you'll get better, more polished as you go along), and learn to tout your positive assets: your appearance, your dependability, your willingness to learn, your financial need (some employers don't want dilettantes who "really don't need the money" and are working for a lark). Most important is the acquisition of a marvelous trait which is called in Yiddish, "chutzpah!" The poor soul has a poor chance on the job market. Hold your head up and your shoulders back and remember, you're doing your employer a favor if he hires you.

Jobs: As Therapy

A job not only provides money, it produces a framework for your life—an important imposition that says you must be somewhere for a specified time every day. No chance for you to wander around your house or apartment aimlessly, watching soaps that are as sad as your own life, or listening to his favorite records while you have a comforting lunchtime martini, or taking a couple of tranquilizers so you can drift and/or sleep through the day.

Pat, now 62, was widowed at 59, after thirty-three years of marriage. She had always worked as a sales clerk, and after her husband died, she took a week off to straighten out her affairs before returning to her old job. She only works part-time now, however, because if she were to earn over $2,700, she would lose her Social Security benefits.

Although Pat received some insurance of her husband's that could supplement her income, the main reason she works is, "I would go crazy without anyone to talk to all day long. I get dressed, put make-up on, and look forward to my job. Some of my customers have been coming to the store for years, so they're friends and we always chat a little. Besides, it keeps my brain sharp to deal with money and prices." I should mention that Pat's brain is so sharp that in slow moments at the store you'll find her doing *The New York Times'* crossword puzzle—in ink!

But it's not only average women who are troubled by loneliness and regard a job as good therapy. Kitty Carlisle, whose husband Moss Hart, the famous playwright, died in 1961, went back to her original theater work even though she had two young children to look after. "I discovered it made me more interesting to my friends. If you're not interesting, no one wants to be bothered with you," she says. Earning money was not her object either, since Miss Carlisle inherited a very significant estate of $1.4 million.

Jobs: What to Do If You Don't Need One

There are widows who can't go to work, because of young kids, and those who don't have to. In these cases, it is important to organize some job-substitute. Establish a meaningful weekday schedule that you will enjoy and stay with, whether it's volunteer work that is creative and satisfying or pooling babysitting time with a neighbor so you can take a course or two that will eventually boost you back into a job or contribute to your personal growth and pleasure.

Joyce Brothers urges action. "For women who haven't been trained for anything, it's vital to do volunteer work or return to college. The universities are reaching out for older women who want to renew their studies or careers. It is crucially important to find some way of getting outside normal household activities."

If you've spent years thinking only of your family, with the highpoint of the day being the time your husband came home and sat down to a wonderful dinner, you must change that focus once and for all. This same re-focusing is required of women who have given up their lives "for the children," who will inevitably grow up and fly away from the nest.

Jobs and Children

Children who have lost their father may feel doubly deserted if suddenly their mother is not around and some strange housekeeper, or even grandmother, is doing all the parenting. Any job considerations, except those of the most urgent financial consequences, should be based on this fly in the ointment.

This can be a real trap. In my own case, for example, I can earn just about enough money to take care of us by working at home—ideal in terms of being with my children and getting the most out of what I earn. But I spend the greatest percentage of my time talking to my typewriter instead of real people. I feel that I should get out in the world if I'm going to remain sane, that I must relate to *adults* with common interests.

But this would be disastrous for the kids, especially the youngest, and financially stupid for me, because by the time I pay for a housekeeper, the clothes needed to replace my normal working outfit of my most comfortable worn-out jeans, transportation, lunches, income taxes, and other expenses, I would probably be earning *less* than if I were to continue freelancing at home.

There are, however, ways of getting out of or around the trap: part-time jobs, child-care set-ups in which instead of feeling deserted a young child will feel special, night-time jobs, and jobs to which you can tote your pre-schoolers with you.

Irene, for example, gets her children to bed, leaves

them with a sitter, and then teaches drama classes a few nights a week. Doris found an ad in the paper for a "real estate assistant." When she had her interview, it was clear that the builder wanted someone to cover his new development on weekends from 1:00 P.M. to 5:00 P.M. and three afternoons a week, when his own salesman couldn't be on the job. "Can I take my two kids with me?" she asked. That was just fine with the builder because he was selling houses to families, after all, and a few kids running around would not detract from his family image. In addition, he felt that a woman with children could understand the needs of house-hunting mothers and do a good selling job on the advantages of his model homes.

Beth saw an ad in her Baltimore paper for a full-time sales clerk at an antiques shop. She called her friend MaryLou, a divorcee; they hired a sitter for a few hours; and collectively, they convinced the antiques shop owner that they could each work three days a week—providing him with his full-time help. When MaryLou works, Beth watches the children . . . and on Beth's days at the shop, MaryLou sits. (Beth's seven-year-old is at school full-time and has after school "enrichment" classes three days a week.) Incidentally, the youngsters, both under three, love this arrangement because they have a chance to socialize with a playmate every day of the week—except Sunday! Remember that Shakespeare sonnet?

> *When in disgrace with fortune and men's eyes,*
> *I all alone beweep my outcast state,*
> *And trouble deaf heaven with my bootless cries*
> *And look upon myself and curse my fate . . .*

I've always loved those lines, but they don't apply to us right now. This is not the time to beweep your state—with booted *or* bootless cries; nor must you curse your fate, which only leads to destructive self-pity.

There is a job waiting for you out there—a meaningful, remunerative occupation that you can make into something special. I can't dismiss the value of that old saw: "Seek and ye shall find."

7 | *Where Did All the Friends Go?*

Some cynical comic once observed, "With friends like this, who needs enemies?" That phrase is all too true and not a bit funny to many widows who find that real friends are rare indeed, especially after the initial flurry of solicitous attention.

As Mary-Anne said, "When you become a widow is when you find out who your real friends are."

Elizabeth Drew, a college classmate, journalist, and author of *Washington Journal: The Events of 1973-1974*, was widowed in 1970, after six years of marriage. Although she doesn't discuss her husband's suicide or her personal life, she is grateful for the friends who helped her through a bad time. "People were incredible, really, the way they rallied around."

Shortly after Alex died, it was wonderful to get a note

105

from a friend saying, "Don't forget we're only a phone call and one and a half hours away. If you get the galloping lonelies, you have only to call and/or come."

Janet remembers, "My friends were all there, right after the funeral, and for a few weeks later; but I don't know, they just seemed to drift away for the most part."

The first friends to become scarcer than hen's teeth are usually the married couples who were "so close." Maureen, who was widowed at 37 with two children under five, told me, "Although we didn't have a lot of friends, we thought we had four or five couples we were really close to. We spent so many weekend nights together, and if my neighbors had been to a party, they thought nothing of dropping in on us at 1:00 A.M. to have a nightcap. After Rob died, I still kept my 'welcoming' lights on outside, but my friends never came over. Although we all used to have dinner together often during the year, now no one invites me. I really became an un-person, as Orwell would say."

Estelle is bitter: "I've lived on this same street for ten years and Joe's been dead for four of those years, but right after he died it was as if I had strangers for neighbors. All the people we used to have drinks with or play a game of cards with suddenly didn't seem to know me. Most of the friends I have now are other outcasts of the town—the divorcees and other widows. But I still can't get over the fact that those old friends just about say hello when I see them on the street."

In their book, *Up From Grief,* Bernadine Kreis and Alice Pattie recognize this reaction; "When you grieve, try not to feel bitter when you lose the friendship of a few persons who are not grief-oriented. If they have visited you or called once and then made the mistake of waiting for you to call . . . they just do not realize that you have lost your initiative. How I wish everyone would learn the enormous effort it takes a new griever just to exist . . .

Good friends take the initiative for as long as you lack it."

Some writers who have turned their attention to the plight of widows think that this kind of ostracism is based on the widow now being a threat to the wife—she might steal the husband. Rita had this type of experience. "Although friends would invite me out to dinner with them, you'd be surprised how many of the women were jealous and thought I was flirting with their husbands. They think, oh there's a young widow and she's going to go after my husband, and that's the least thing you want to do. So you can't stay with the same crowd of friends you had before."

Alice's friends were wonderful "immediately, for comfort," she says. "But when I moved to Florida I had to make new friends, and this was difficult because I was seldom included in things. I seemed to pose a threat. In some ways I still do."

Other writers, taking a more feminist tack, say a widow is a threat to the *husband* because she proves that a woman can make it on her own without the assistance of a man. There is probably a little bit of truth in both these views; personally, I feel most married friends drop you because they don't know what to do with you!

Adelle agrees with me and says, "Friends would like to help, I'm sure, but they don't really know how because they don't know if you're going to jump out a window, burst into tears, get into an argument, or what."

Some widows expressed a quite different problem with "old" friends. "I never realized so many of the people we knew were really my *husband's* acquaintances," says Carla. "After Tom died, and they made all the proper responses—good friendly ones, I don't mean to be bitter —it was like a door closing. I just wasn't included in things."

Gloria and her husband had lived in seven different

cities in the sixteen years they were married. "For all those years, most of the friends I made were through Jeff's company or business connections. After he died I decided to stay here (a suburb of Philadelphia), but it's tough going because I'm so lonely. There's a real difference between being a company wife and an unattached widow."

Sally found that friends did rally around and that in most cases, if someone was having a party where she and Howard would have been invited, she was invited anyway. "But this wasn't so fifteen years ago when I was divorced and lived in this same community. Maybe it was because I didn't know the people as well, or maybe it's the difference in status. But I don't think being divorced or widowed was the reason, really. I think my friends have grown in their understanding of what it is like to be alone."

My own experience with couples parallels Maureen's, except that I found that instead of being totally dropped, I was asked to *lunch* by the wives of formerly close couples. Eager for crumbs, I would arrange such a meeting maybe once a month, but lunch time is not particularly when one gets the blues. It's the long evenings, especially on weekends, when you would love to have a few rousing laughs and some good talk, not just woman-to-woman, but people-to-people.

At some point I decided I was getting psychotic about it all and instead of waiting for invitations, I should issue some of my own. So I called one couple who had been very friendly for years. They came to dinner on a Friday night, but instead of it turning into one of the 2:00 or 3:00 A.M. talkfests I had known, they became tired about midnight and left. We had had a good time, but it wasn't the same. Of course it couldn't be, and maybe we were all awkward and nervous by Alex's absence.

I was lucky enough to have one good pair of friends

who were with me all through my husband's illness. They stayed with me the night he died, took me out to dinner on several occasions afterward, got tickets for shows, involved themselves with my children, and were super throughout. Doris and Lee are the exception that proves the rule: one of those givens we spoke of earlier is that you will pretty much have to scratch the old-friend list. This given has a solution: you must make new friends. Easier said than done. But they are around you if you look.

I found some right under my nose—through my children. While gnashing my teeth and biting my nails, two couples emerged who were the parents of my children's best friends. Nobody sought anybody. It all happened naturally because of the kids, and possibly would have occurred if Alex were still alive . . . but then again, possibly not. What makes both these friendships so good is that they didn't know Alex well, and therefore they dealt with me as a person, not as Alex's wife-turned-widow, and without the awkwardness of realizing that someone is missing. Maybe it was luck. In any case, both these couples often ask me over for a drink on Saturday night (knowing I don't need a sitter because I'm just going down the street), or invite me to a party (even though everyone else there will be in pairs, but I might have a good time anyway—and I do).

In turn, I've reciprocated and spent some entertaining and fulfilling evenings with them *chez moi*, feeling like a person, full-fledged, and engaging on my own. A couple of couples don't fill the void, however, and it's unhealthy to rely totally on married friends.

The problem with too much two-by-two socializing was illustrated by an incident Lorraine remembered. "A group of couples used to go away for weekends together. At some point one man's wife died, and the husband of one couple wanted to include him on a weekend trip. His wife said, 'Why should he come? He doesn't belong with us anymore. We're all couples!' When I became a widow, her words stuck in my head and I certainly wouldn't impose myself on them."

Instead, Lorraine actively changed her life; she joined clubs, a bowling group, and became very active in different charitable organizations. "I had to make new friends; there was no room for me with the old ones."

Tina had a similar experience at a party with some married couples she hadn't seen since Peter died. "Although I was the only single person there, it was a lovely evening until someone mentioned the 'disaster' at their last gourmet club dinner. I was interested because I've taken some courses in gourmet food, but when I asked about it, my friends changed the subject quickly. Afterwards I realized it was because they felt bad that they hadn't included me in their club—it was open only to couples, after all."

Marian, who still lives in the handsome, lake-view Chicago apartment she and her husband bought some years ago, says, "When I spend an evening with a married couple, there's always that point when if I talk about my troubles—whether it's dates, money, or loneliness—I know they feel uncomfortable, although they are tremendously sympathetic to my need to talk. And when they go home, to what I know is the bed they'll share together, and maybe make love, but certainly be close to each other, *I* feel uncomfortable."

"I'll go out with other couples now and then," says Terry, "but it definitely depends on the situation. When it involves a social event where the men are going to be talking together and the women will be off in their own corner, that's fine, but if it's strictly couple-by-couple, I feel uncomfortable."

Rita's reaction was also one of discomfort when a couple invited her to a dinner dance. "I thought I would be sitting at the table with them, but I was put with a group of strangers, mostly married. I really felt awkward and embarrassed."

Gina wishes her old married friends could be a little more sensitive. "We all belong to the same clubs and often there are formal parties that I enjoy going to. But I hate going alone, especially when I'm dressed up in a gown. It seems demeaning to get in the car and drive myself to the affair. If a couple would only say, 'Come on, we'll pick you up.' That would be all I'd want."

Insensitivity was the word used by Carla who feels deserted by her friends. "People who haven't gone through this couldn't care less. They don't want to hear about your tragedy. They want you to turn it off and pretend it never happened . . . and just to make sure they won't hear about it, they drop you."

To Meralle, another California widow, being dropped may well be easier than being tolerated. "Worse than that, there is that 'smile if it kills you,' always reply you are 'fine' and 'buck up' philosophy that forbids expressing loss or loneliness (or even a tear). Rightly or wrongly, the newly widowed begins to feel that people look in the other direction (the clichés are endless) and that the old Indian custom of Purdah (hiding women from the world) would be a kindness."

You can uncover people to talk with at the widow-to-widow programs we talked about in chapter three. But for some women this isn't the answer. "I tried that for a while, with a group at my synagogue," reports Carole. While it was fine as therapy, a "swapping" of experiences, what she really wants is a group of friends that are simpatico. "I want to talk about books I love, or try different new restaurants. I don't want to spend the rest of my life sorting out my problems as a widow."

You have to find kindred spirits—a task rather like looking for a needle in the proverbial haystack. Widows seem to remain in the woodwork (or haystack), even though there are so many of us. One man I met recently automatically assumed I was divorced. A common assumption because people have those built-in "gray-haired" notions of what widows are like. But it is among divorcees, a definitely "higher-profile" group, that you will probably find your most accessible new friends.

The problem is that divorcees also have a somewhat different frame of reference from yours. While you worry about Social Security, managing the house on your own, etc., they are worrying about final decrees, child support, and alimony. While you fret about tombstones, they fret about custody and whether or not the ex-husband (and possibly his new wife) is brainwashing their children.

Aunt Rose is more at home with widows, because "when you're widowed you feel the one you loved is gone, and you're left with love in your heart. Divorcees don't feel this way; they are bitter." Estelle also has trouble relating to divorcees; "Although most of my friends—and that isn't a large number—are divorced, it seems they're always talking about what a stinker their husband is, or why doesn't he send more money, or how he hasn't seen the kids for three weeks. They don't understand that they are lucky to have someone send them money—any amount—or take the kids off their hands. They are always complaining."

Kate doesn't feel very different from divorcees. "Other than not feeling 'rejected,' as they do, we have a lot of the same problems in common. Sometimes I envy women who have never been married. They have no children, no responsibilities to anyone but themselves."

Nora looks at the contrast between widows and divorcees more philosophically. "All the divorces I know of were 'bad' ones, and so the women going through it have a living pain. My situation is so *final*. The questions I have will never be answered, so I put them to rest. Divorcees are still asking why. We're not torn by visitor's rights, nor are we aided by them. Sometimes in a way I think I have it easier. The non-marrieds elude me completely; there is little empathy there."

Still, the subject at hand here is meeting friends, and with divorcees you can compare notes in many areas: problems with children, financial difficulties, and most of all, meeting men, which ultimately becomes a boring subject when all your activities seem motivated in that direction.

Gina was one of the few widows I spoke with who said that most of her friends are widows. "I live in a small town where there are few divorcees. And although I'm fifty-five, my friends call me a kid—they are all five or ten years older. We have fun together, but if a widow wants to talk about her troubles or her dead husband I avoid her. I don't want to be depressed. I have a sister-in-law who still talks about my husband (who died over ten years ago) and tells me how much she misses her wonderful brother. I finally said, 'Look, nobody missed your brother more than I did, but I don't want to talk about it.' "

You need friends to go places with, share experiences with, talk to, on an adult basis, whether they are married friends, divorced, or single. One widow told me the best answer is to have male friends: "Determined bachelors, incipient or overt fags, they will be a super help and provide a strong and understanding shoulder you can lean on. Plus they'll take you to the movies, or go dutch on dinner."

Whatever your choice of friends, when you have few or none your state can be pretty wretched. I talked to Millie on a Sunday afternoon, and she said, "There are times I don't know where to go and what to do. I'm really feeling lonely right now, but today everybody's out and I'm home." Helen is less emotional about it and flatly says, "I don't have a group of friends in my position. Everybody I know is married."

How to meet new friends? It's rather like looking for a job, which, many widows agree, is one of the most natural ways to make good, congenial acquaintances of both sexes. The various widows groups will help too, and the members of such clubs don't always discuss their problems—they like to have fun as well. Tina made friends by joining a beginner's tennis class: "It took me two months to get around to doing this, but once I did, I found tennis was terrific exercise, and the class has led to an entirely different social life."

Golf was Eve's solution. "I couldn't afford to join a private club, but there was a public course nearby and I lucked into a threesome the first time out, a group which seemed to know a lot of the other players. Over a period of two or three years I met maybe twelve or fifteen friends that I would see outside the golf course."

Irene chose to search where her career interests were. "I made strong efforts in the theatre, in the community, and at the university. I joined a theatre group, started acting again, taught some classes in drama. I enjoyed what I was doing and I think this makes you more receptive to meeting new people."

This feeling is echoed by Anne, who found friends by working in politics. "I've always been a strong Democrat, but I had never participated in local or national campaigns. When I volunteered to work at the county office, I was told I'd spend a lot of time licking stamps and addressing envelopes—and I did. But I was also an insider and got into strategy and discussions, and met a lot of people who feel the same way about government as I do."

Some widows find the need for companionship is most apparent when it involves traveling. Jessica has a coterie of divorced friends who she sees often, but they aren't free to travel. "Or, if they are, they don't want the same trips that I do. And this is when I really miss my husband. But I don't like the idea of going off on my own."

I told Jessica about a fairly new group called the "Widows Travel Club" (see Appendix VI) accidentally organized by travel agent Beatrice Green, when she tried to help a widowed friend by pairing her with another widow she knew for a vacation trip. Bea is remarried now, but she was widowed in her twenties with two young children, so she is very empathetic to the problems of women *sans* husbands. Her first travel "match" was so successful that she began to introduce other like-minded widows to each other. The idea mushroomed: today there are about 4,000 members of the "Widows Travel Club" and she has personally paired off about 300 widows. This kind of club can provide compatible contacts both at home and abroad. Members fill out questionnaires on their personal habits and other pertinent information—age, smoking, drinking habits, the type of trip they want to take, entertainment, food preferences, and length of vacation.

Aside from the idea of companionship, Mrs. Green points out that people who travel alone are financially penalized for their single status. For proof, just check the single surcharge on travel bureau folders. "Even on guided tours, a single woman is at a sharp disadvantage. She must pay almost the same money for accommodations as a couple pays . . . And then psychologically, she must face that time usually seven in the evening when the tour activities break up and she is left alone for dinner and the rest of the night . . . And if a widow is on tour with other husbands and wives, however kind these couples try to be, the widow will feel excluded."

Most of us, however, would agree that existing friends could be a little more understanding, resourceful, imaginative, and faithful. It is definitely true that those who have had some tragedy—divorce, widowhood, or some other accident of fate—are more ready to help another get back into a social scene. Some months ago I found myself doing the giving and getting some rewards for my "altruism." Thanksgiving was approaching and I dreaded still another holiday without Alex, trapped into the family dinners that had now become simply something one must get through. I was having lunch with Nancy and I asked her about Thanksgiving plans. She had none, so I invited her and her young son to dinner. Then the spirit really took over and I decided to invite a divorced friend and her two children.

Because I didn't want this to be a "ladies only" party, I called Alex's best friend whom I hadn't seen for a year, a Canadian member of Parliament who was in New York for a few months, and a man I had dated but wasn't really interested in. I also extended the usual invitation to my family. I cooked for four days—the first time since Alex died that I was interested in a party. And it was a good party. My single friends all called me afterward to tell me what a wonderful time they had had. My family stopped discussing family matters and put on their social graces. All the children had an absolute ball. And although I was exhausted afterward, it was a marvelous feeling to know I had spread a little happiness around—and had enjoyed myself as well.

"Friendship, friendship, what a perfect blendship," sing Frank Sinatra and Bing Crosby in the movie, *High Society*. There aren't that many perfect blends, but I think it's rather like digging for gold. If you keep on with it, you'll find your lode. Not overnight, but eventually. Sitting and fretting about your life won't do it. You have to really dig.

Attitude is a factor, too. If you act like a pathetic bereft wretch, friends will think of you as a burden instead of a boon, and will unconsciously drift away. Nobody wants to feel *obligated* to invite you to dinner or a party. The more independent you are, and the more people you begin to see as a person in your own right, the better your chance for maintaining some of those old friendships, and making new ones. You must go beyond the role of a lonely, single woman, because this is not enough to sustain *friendship*. You have to be comfortable with yourself before others will be comfortable with you, and we'll be talking about this self-security in chapter ten.

8 | Sinking or Swimming: The Singles Scene

If you were a product of the uptight fifties and now find yourself adrift, all alone, in the turbulent sea of the swinging seventies, not only have you come a long way, baby, but you have a long way to go!

Life is very different out there now, and although you may have been vaguely aware of this, or more specifically tuned into the sexual revolution in terms of your teenage children, or even so aware that you read *The Joy of Sex* (twice), awareness *of* and participation *in* are two very different things. The next chapter concerns your reintroduction to the sex act itself, but since it takes two to tangle, right now our attention is to meeting the men you will tangle with.

Although some of the old ways are still operative (blind dates, for example), the new ways are challenging, frus-

119

trating, but often necessary, and this includes the questionable institution of singles bars, the benevolent formation of singles groups, the mechanized aspect of computer dating and matchmaking, and a quite varied selection of approaches in which lonely people are supposed to meet the temporary or permanent mate of their dreams.

Plunging into this bewildering situation is loaded with emotional trauma. But after bravely crossing the threshold into the new world, the *experiences* you'll have are something else again.

To Dr. Brothers, these experiences are indeed important in shaping your new life. "Take any invitation that comes along. Anything. Cut through your reservations and try different approaches. You'll learn as you go along, and anything is better than sitting in front of a television set."

For most widows, the first step is feeling *when* it is right to date again, not so much *who* the lucky man will be. (And if the who is right, but the when is wrong, the fateful meeting may never take place.) Gina apologized, "Maybe this sounds terrible, but although people mean well, they can cause harm by giving your number to people too soon, or to people you won't like. I told a good friend I really wasn't ready, but she did give a man my name and phone number anyway, and he was so persistent I finally went out with him. But we spent most of the evening talking about my dead husband and his dead wife."

For some widows there is never a right time. Pat says, "I had a happy marriage, and although I've been propositioned, I'm just not interested in going out with anybody." It does seem that the longer one was married, the less interested she is in dating, sex, or even eventual remarriage.

Karen's mother was widowed at fifty-seven. "Mom simply is not concerned about getting married again, and

I think her attitude is that she was so happy with my father, another marriage is unnecessary. She's active and busy, but she doesn't have the same motivation as say I do or you do. But it isn't that she's shy or anti-social."

One aunt of mine did admit to being shy and not very sociable. After Alex died, Aunt Mary said to me, "I made a mistake ten years ago when I was still young enough and attractive enough to marry again. When Uncle Charlie died and I started going out with my lady friends, there were some widowers who would come over to our table, and try to be friendly, maybe even ask me to dance. But I would always lower my head or look away and not give them any encouragement. I realize now how wrong that was but I just didn't think anyone could measure up to my husband. Now I see that I could have made another man a good wife, and I would have been happier myself."

Aunt Rose recalls, "In all these years I've never thought about it. It never seemed like a reasonable possibility. There were so many problems, and I was busy with Anthony (her son) and happy that I was able to take care of us."

In a word, many widows are "contented with my fate." But a good majority of those who are fifty-five and younger are not so ready to accept celibacy and singlehood for the last third of their lives. According to new figures, the average married woman can expect to live eighteen years as a widow. This may not seem frightening to those whose husbands are still alive, but to widows this statistic represents all too grim reality.

The widows who would like to remarry usually started dating from three to six months after their husbands died. And usually they eased into it the first time by "doubling" with another couple, or arranging a softer social situation that would not seem as much like the teenage equivalent of dating.

Karen had her first date six months after Bob died, a

dinner engagement set up with another couple. "Afterwards," she says, "we went back to their house and had a drink or two and then I drove myself home. It wasn't a problem of having to say goodnight at the front door to a 'date.' "

Lorraine arranged to meet her first date—a blind date who had heard about her from a friend—outside of her church, after confession. "But I tell you, before I got into his car, I really felt like jumping into my own car and driving home fast." In a "first the good news, now the bad news" story, Lorraine ultimately married the man, only to become a widow again several years later.

'Once the *when* is settled, you can seek the *who*, but for many widows this is a problem because of their very identity. Here is the area where the differences between widows and divorcees is probably most apparent. Divorcees have the advantage of the cleansing emotion of anger directed at their exhusbands, a nice strong emotion that acts as a protective shield and gives them some trump cards you don't have. Another plus, if such circumstances can be seen as advantages, is pointed out by Dr. Brothers. "Divorcees have participated in the decision to end a marriage, willingly or not, and usually this has not been thrust upon her as a *fait accompli*. All a widow can fall back on is a range of confused emotions and despair at something that happened beyond her control."

Widows have to come off as ex- happily married women. You can't admit, even if it was true, that the dear departed was a son-of-a-bitch. And if you happened to have had a good marriage, this really operates against you.

As one man I met stated, "You inhibit me." I never thought of such a thing, but then he explained, "You loved your husband, so I feel you're measuring me against him. With a divorcee this isn't so. If he left her, she's so angry, I'll beat any comparison. If she left him, it was because he was a loser in some way. So my ego stands up with divorcees."

Now, this was a kind man, and someone I'd like to spend more time with, and all I could say was that if I felt I could only love one person, I would only have had one child; ergo . . .

In contrast, however, I met another man who strongly disagrees. "I think widows are *safe*," he emphasized. "They actually loved someone and were true to him and still are, but divorcees come off as women incapable of love, or as rather bitchy ladies, and they frighten me."

Joyce Brothers recognizes this confusion in attitudes. "Men have to understand the difference between widows and divorcees, and unfortunately, all too often, they don't. Widows are more open to love relationships than divorcees; they can transfer this affection to someone else. They have known a meaningful and satisfying relationship and can more readily identify with the emotion, impact, and implications of loving than a divorcee who is distrustful because of her bad experience."

In the singles world, it may seem logical to lump "gay" divorcees and "merry" widows together. And in one sense we belong together: there are forty-nine million of us: men and women, widows and widowers, the divorced and legally separated, and those who have never married, ranging in age from recent college graduates to retired people. As a statistical group we represent almost one-quarter of our country's population. Anyone for "Single Power"? But having been both divorced and widowed, I realize there is a vast difference in roles. Divorcees may not be particularly gay (just as widows aren't notably merry), but they are more readily *accepted*. The death of a marriage is easier to cope with socially than the death of a mate.

There are other differences: divorcees are often eager to marry again, to prove they can succeed in the role. Divorcees say, "I will do better." Widows, even those who would like to remarry, say, "I might do worse." And with this kind of attitude they are likely to "flaunt" the successful, though now defunct, marriage and therefore drive potential suitors away.

The widows I talked to all admitted to "nervousness" about dating that was quite different from anything they had known in the long ago "real" single days.

On her first time out with a man, Alice "blabbed incessantly, to exorcise the ghost." "I wanted an audience to dramatize his death to, over and over again, thereby, somehow realizing my own life. The first man and then other men became sounding boards, not people. It was a long time before I realized I really hoped to keep them away."

Beth was nevous about wanting to have dates while still wanting to be alone. "I learned early to say goodnight to those who were a bore and even to those who weren't. I really, truly wanted to be alone. I sipped my gin, I watched my TV, I read my book, I took care of my kids, and I craved time."

Cathy's edginess about dates led her to drive herself to and from appointments. "I needed isolation, and the sense that I could leave whenever I chose to. This changed, though, in later years (she's been a widow for six years), and I have enjoyed the shared responsibility of meeting. I don't think that will change again. I do like being picked up and dropped off, or at least escorted home."

The aspect of meeting a date under your own steam is one that concerns a good many "dating" widows, who are at odds with the convention that single ladies should insist on an escort to take them home. Terry, who lives in a Boston suburb, gets almost angry with this attitude. "If I go to a party in town, I drive in, or even if I don't drive and somebody drops me off, how can I ask a man without a car to schlep me all the way out to the suburbs, by cab or subway? It's unfair and unrealistic."

There are also suburban widows who drive themselves to parties where eligible dates most logically have their own cars. So there you are with two cars. Adelle said, "One of the most chivalrous things that's happened to me as a widow, and there haven't been many, is that a man I met insisted on following me home with *his* car to make sure I got there safely." Once home, Adelle did the chivalrous thing and asked him in for a drink.

I've been driving in and out of New York for the last twenty years, and I am not unused to driving by myself. But lately, not only does the city make me nervous, but I judge whether or not a social event is worth the effort on balance against that lonely drive home. It's not so much that I'm afraid of being mugged or raped (which I am), or the idea that if I've had one gin and tonic too many, I'll have an accident, with the resulting horror that my children could become orphans, but really, the very sad feeling of getting myself home—home to my empty bed, my quiet house. That drive home is more depressing, at times, than actually *staying* home and watching television or reading, which I'm now accustomed to doing.

Getting to and fro isn't the only problem voiced by widows who are nervous about dates. "I find myself drifting off sometimes, wondering what I'm doing here smiling politely at this boring man," says Amy, now forty-eight, who lives alone in Detroit. JoAnne is nervous about wanting to please. "After an easy-going married relationship, there's pressure trying to be a 'good date' as it were. Sometimes I think back on some of the things I've said and I feel as if I acted like a zoony, to use my daughter's word. I'm trying so hard to be *on*!"

JoAnne is nervous about how she looks. "When I go out, sometimes I ask my children four or five times if I look okay. Of course they always say 'great.' But what

I'm doing is making up for the one time I would have asked my husband—who would have said 'great'—and he isn't around."

It's not surprising, then, that with these pressures, some widows develop their own anger, ultimately not so different in kind from that of the divorcee. "How could he do this to me!"

Psychologists say hostility is often a more comfortable alternative than facing the reality of the emptiness of death or accepting the idea that one is a victim of fate. But most of the widows I talked with denied being angry. Some of them directed their anger at other people: the driver of the car that caused the fatal accident, the employer that fired the husband who then died of stress, the doctors who didn't pull off a miracle.

"Yet," says Helen, "this is really anger at *the husband* for desertion. It's just that divorced women have a real person to be angry at and widows can't be angry at the person who isn't there. It's also hard to come to terms with the anger because widows have idealized the husband."

This is not a situation that affects widows only. Widowers have much the same reaction, and this may be the reason why so many widows and widowers can have one good date where both parties cry in their beer and compare notes on those who have died. But follow-up interest isn't necessarily there.

When I mentioned to Annette the friend who talked about my inhibiting him, she said, "I never thought of this, but now it seems to me that in some way, the first man I went out with—a widower—was looking at me and comparing me to his wife. But most of the men I dated afterwards were divorced and had had unhappy experiences, so maybe they thought I didn't have as bad a situation. I wasn't angry at anybody."

Aside from this plethora of unsettling attitudes that

pull and tear and cause confusion in the widow who does want to date and meet men, there is the problem of dealing with the men she will meet, who by type include *The Ideal Man, The Younger Man, The Married Man, The Divorced Man*, and *The Rogue*. All of these types can be encountered at any of the social outlets that will be discussed, but four of them merit special attention: the Ideal, the Young, the Married, and the Divorced. The Rogue, of course, can belong to any of these categories. And it should be pointed out that the roles often overlap, so that you may have an ideal man who is at once married and younger, or a young man who is ideal but a rogue, or a divorced man who is ideal, and so on.

The Ideal Man

The idealization of the dead husband is a definite hang-up. As psychologist Martin Sylvester explained, "This makes the social situation tough for both the widow and the man, and the man senses this." One date told Helen, who is also a therapist, "This is a hard act to follow." And Marilyn observed, "The best husband is a dead husband. So often the man becomes a saint after he dies. You forget about all the fights, all the acrimony, and remember only the good times."

What do I remember about Alex? Aside from the love and sex, aside from how marvelous he was as a father, aside from the fact that we shared the same interests in books, movies, art, I remember that he made me *laugh*. I haven't found this talent in anyone else I've met, and I search for it constantly. There have been times when I've made a date laugh, and I revel in this, and then wait to laugh in return. It doesn't happen. I tell myself not to make comparisons, but that's like telling Sandy to eat his spinach—an impossibility.

If finding a new mate were like eating in a Chinese restaurant, we could take one from column A and one from

column B and one from column C and put them all together and they would spell love, and/or husband, depending on your goals. I've not been able to pull it all
together and find one person to satisfy my appetite. Yet, I
know I am idealizing a good many of Alex's characteristics, and this is dangerous socially and mentally.

Karen says, "It's not that I have a check list of Bob's
traits and I say if you don't come through on eight out of
ten of these, it's no good. I don't really want to compare.
But I do have a specific set of ideas of what makes a man
good for me—and this is crucial. There are certain quali-
ties I realize I need."

I say "amen," to that, and I have to agree with Sarah
who says she mentions her late husband on dates. "I don't
deliberately bring him up out of a clear blue sky, but I
don't go out of my way *not* to talk about him. If it
comes up, I tell what it was like with Hal. I want a date
to know that I was fortunate enough to have someone I
loved and respected and admired. I don't have to get
married for financial reasons, but I'd like to get married
again, so when I make comparisons, it's really a way of
saying the man is as nice as Hal was."

Deirdre's ideal has changed in the ten years she's been
widowed. "I was always attracted to tall, football-player
types, but at this age, my age, they've become overweight;
all that muscle has turned to flab. So now, physically, I
like tall, lean men. But I've also been involved with short,
fat, bald men who responded to other psychological
needs."

Imaginative and creative men are the ideal of Gloria,
who describes her husband, Jeff, as being very creative although very erratic about money. "Even though I can't
live that way, I still respond to the adventurous spirit of
men like that."

When a woman has lived with a man for a number of
years, it is impossible to wipe out the enduring effects of

that relationship. If you were happy, you look for the same things that will make you happy again, whether it's appearance, outlook, personality, economic position, a way with children, a similar age and background—the whole wrap-up. Although it may seem sensible, it also sets up the groundwork for precluding other meaningful relationships as well. While the divorced woman may be looking for someone quite different, the widow is usually looking for someone just the same. And that is a very complicated problem.

The Younger Man

While conducting these interviews, I was amazed at a social situation that popped up almost unanimously among widows, or at least the ones who are interested in dating: the younger man. There seem to be several disparate explanations for his ubiquitous presence.

Perhaps the most important reason is that widows try very hard to look attractive, a trait they hold in common with divorcees, but one that may well be encouraged by the need to defy that gray-haired stereotype again. Because they try harder, they are often rewarded by the attentions of younger men, who have no idea what their real age is.

Helen expressed another reason. "I always tended to date older men when I was younger. Now I find that I date men closer to my own age. Maybe it's the idea that an older man might die. There's that fear, once it's happened to you. You don't want to take a chance on it happening again."

Marilyn describes a third possibility. "Availability. The men who are around fifty seem to want younger women; the men around sixty are a little too old for me; and the men my own age are already married. So the field is open to those in their thirties who are recently divorced or haven't ever married."

Polly Bergen, who is divorced, said much the same thing recently, in explaining why she was dating a twenty-six-year-old man. "The people [men] my own age are either married or involved with younger women." In one sense, cheers for Polly, but in another, the situation is not quite so simple.

How do widows react to younger men? Not as unanimously as they note his presence in the social scene. For Karen and Nancy, both of whom have sons in their twenties, the situation is almost "ludicrous." Karen recounted the story of meeting a twenty-nine-year-old man on a vacation. While she considered it only a casual encounter, he tracked down her hotel, and asked for a date the following night. "I was hysterical. I'm so used to playing mother to David's friends, that I couldn't possibly take him seriously."

Nancy is not so much amused as bemused. "It really is flattering and nice to look very young, but not so much fun when they are so young they are like babies. They don't know the same radio programs I grew up with; they haven't seen the same movies. We actually don't have very much in common."

But this isn't the only problem. Nancy continues, "I agreed to have a drink with a young neighbor just to be friendly. But then he pursued it, and after turning him down quite a few times, I agreed once more. During our talk I mentioned my son Mike, who is now twenty-six, and this guy was absolutely shocked. I mean shocked. He said 'That's terrible. How awful for you.' Obviously I never saw him again. Imagine that having a son so grown-up could be considered awful!"

Martha is 54 and currently dating a man seven years younger. "Although he's very protective of me and doesn't act younger, I still feel maternal toward him, and I've never had any children, but he still causes that response."

On the other hand, Tina doesn't mind going with

younger men "if they are stimulating enough intellectually and if they are succeeding at whatever they do. I like successful men; I find they are more interesting than, say, someone just starting out in his career. At fifty-one, I don't want to struggle through life again with a man just at the beginning of his profession. I want someone content with himself, satisfied with what he's doing."

I'm very flattered that men think I'm 34, or 35, or 36, and, of course, the fact that I have fairly young children contributes to this belief. But once the flattery is done with, I'm frankly bored by young men. The eight-year spread between Alex and me was a *plus* in many ways, and as I grew older I could catch up to him to the point where although I hadn't seen "It Happened One Night" in a theater, I had seen it often enough on TV to share it with him. But an eight-year-age difference with younger men is a minus for me. Not only are too many of them unimpressed with Colbert and Gable, but they are turned off by the Adlai Stevenson cult, or the McCarthy debacle, or the game show scandals. They know about the West Coast Dodgers and Giants, not the famous days of Ebbetts Field and the Polo Grounds. They know, but it's a form of history, and I am not ready yet to become a history teacher. I crave mutual interests, likes, memories. I would like to joke about victory gardens, ration stamps, letters to G.I.s, S.W.A.K. (although I wasn't even a teenager), and Jo Stafford singing, "I'd Like To Get You On a Slow Boat to China," but someone five, six, eight years younger than I doesn't even know who Jo Stafford was, much less remember that slow boat, or the stamps, or the gardens, or the letters we kids sent off to our "fighting men." The things that were real for me are "trivia" for younger men.

Also, and this may peg me as an old-fashioned lady, there is something about the way our world is set up that makes it easier for older men to connect to younger women—à la Bing Crosby, Dean Martin, Aristotle Onassis, Stavros Niarchos, Pablo Picasso, Pablo Casals, Henry Fonda, and Henry Ford. But *younger* men— younger? Merle Oberon seems to be pulling it off with her husband who is twenty years her junior. Anouk Aimee, Jeanne Moreau, Brigitte Bardot, Ava Gardner, Liz Taylor, and even a Woolworth heiress or two are ready to do this.

But if your main goal is not the pursuit of youth, a man significantly your junior could turn out to be a less than comfortable choice. And aside from the lack of common experiences, do you really want to be somebody's pseudo-mother, or run the rat race of staying as young looking as your mate?

Four of the widows I interviewed had been seriously involved with younger men, and they are the exception that disproves all my feelings. Tanya will eventually marry her man, who is 32 to her 41. "I never feel older than Jack," she said. "In fact, he makes me feel younger. It's as if I have a chance to recapture a decade of my life, the thirties, when I spent so many miserable years."

Cara-Sue dated a man six years younger for about a year and was very close to marrying him. "On a one-to-one relationship we had no problems about the age difference, but what began to get to me were Will's friends. He was twenty-six, and some in his crowd were twenty-four or twenty-five. A few were still in grad school, and their dates were either in college or brand new graduates. At thirty-two, I felt really out of it, and they were uncomfortable with my position as a widow. I think in their eyes I might just as well have been forty-two!"

An eight-year difference is no problem to Estelle who has been dating Ray very seriously for four months. "My husband was four-and-a-half years younger, so I seem to be attracted to younger men. I worry that our age difference bothers Ray, especially since he's never been married. Not only would he become a husband, but he would be an instant father to a twelve-year-old and an eight-year-old. He wants to marry me, but I'm the one who's hesitating." Then, with a very contented smile, she added, "But not too much."

The seven-year gap between Jill and Gary is "no problem at all. I'm happy now for the first time since Bill died; Billy Jr. relates to Gary beautifully, and we interact like a happy family. I don't know if marriage is in the cards or not, but the age difference is not something that either of us think too much about."

The Married Man

"The hell with it. Who am I to supervise or worry about someone else's marriage? I'm interested in this man and I like him and I'm going to get pleasure out of this relationship. I've become much more selfish. If there's trouble with his marriage, I haven't started it."

Ellen's statement was blunt, hard, tough. Not really in keeping with the image I had of her from our long talks together. But her explanation softened the impact: "Look, I would never purposely break up anyone's marriage, but Richard just can't hack it with his wife anymore. She has her tennis and bridge and the kids, and they don't even talk these days. Something happened a long time ago and he's lonely, as lonely as I am. I know he'll never get a divorce, that he won't marry me, and that we won't live happily ever after.

"But in the meantime, I'm not living happily now—with anyone. Is it too much to ask to be happy once a week, when we can spend some time together?"

It wasn't really a rhetorical question. It deserved an answer. No—that isn't too much to ask. That happens to be my opinion, and I can't say it represents any solid percentage of American widows. Most of the ones I confronted with the question, "Would you (could you) get involved with a married man?", answered "no" immediately. And then a good number of them qualified it by saying, "It all depends on the circumstances."

Perhaps widows in general are what my mother calls "goody-goody"—all too ready to provide sympathy when presented with a sad story. And a great many firmly married men have sad stories to tell. Or perhaps, in reaching out for affection, for love, if a good man comes along, it doesn't matter if you can't have him full-time. It's better to have something rather than nothing, as Ellen concluded. And maybe the answer is a combination of both reasons. And maybe it just depends on the man.

I have almost mounted soapboxes in my avid condemnation of married men who fool with single ladies. I have preached about this at parties. I have been cruel to the few married men who crossed my path under less than honest auspices. In fact, I'm still sardonically amused at the lesson I taught one unsuspecting husband, who with great anticipation, drove all the way home with me—in my car—only to get as far as my kitchen where I pointed to the telephone and suggested he phone for a cab home to Watchung, New Jersey, that I knew would cost him a cool forty bucks! I don't like married men who are out on the town for a night and return home, hungover, sexually gratified, to mow their lawns and play the attentive daddy and husband the next day. Not over my still alive body.

But, in my brief time as a single, I have met one married man for whom I set aside my rantings and railings about cheaters and sneaks. It is true that I said I wouldn't play a Fannie Hurst *Back Street* scene, but while it lasted, the relationship restored my belief in the male half of the human race, and provided a good bit of comfort for my head, and, if you will, my soul.

However, other widows have been burned with the shibboleth expressed by one erstwhile husband who was, ironically, trying to score with me: "Never believe a married man. He'll love you and leave you."

Anita, Terry, Marilyn, Carole, JoAnne, Tina, Nancy, and Karen are a few of the widows who have been burned, but their experiences were on a short-range, one-night-stand basis. Sarah, Anne, and Virginia followed the same route as Ellen and I, and of the five of us, Ellen is still seeing her married man.

Ultimately, we found I couldn't continue the relationship—not for moral reasons, but because of the children, who were becoming too attached to Don. "Will you be my new father?" asked Robbie, a hope shared but unspoken by Maria and Sandy. Since Don was still committed to his marriage, there was no way he could fill this role on a long-term basis. Neither he nor I wanted the kids to be hurt again, which after all, proved my faith in what a good man he was.

The Divorced Man

Divorce produces the most potential friends of both sexes for widows. But the formerly married man is not as free as he (or society) thinks he is—he has several hang-ups that relate back to his old status that affect his behavior with single women.

One problem is the need to score, if not soar. Anita says, "Sometimes divorced men remind me of birds let out of a cage. They are wild. I wonder what their marriages were like if they have such a need for sex. Oh, it's nice to be wanted sexually, but I feel they are trying to prove something, to count scalps."

Tanya observes, "If I had to rate divorced, widowed, or single men in terms of respect, by the way they behaved, or by what my old Latin teacher would call decorum, I would give the best rating to widowed men, who seem to be a little more old-fashioned. I'm not talking about kissing goodnight on the first date or that old jazz, I'm talking about not being maneuvered into *going to bed* on the first date!"

I have to agree with Tanya on her rating system, possibly for different reasons. The never-married men I've met have been younger and tuned into life as swingers. Nonetheless they have been more or less well-behaved—the first dates, anyway. Perhaps my status as a widow threw them off. With the few widowers I've met, we spent most of the introductory time talking about dead mates, and there hasn't been any follow-up. I think, though, that each of us was somewhat embarrassed at the new sexual roles we were forced to play.

It seems as if divorced men are not so much trying to collect scalps, but rather that they are trying to heal wounds. No matter who initiated the divorce, there are resulting bruises. And finding a congenial woman to go to bed with is good balm for the bruises.

In addition, aside from premature gropings, many divorced men are still "married men" in their souls. They have become accustomed to the convenience of a wife and often treat their dates as such, or would like to. There is also the extreme condition of those who were so turned off by marriage that they live by the code of "once burned, twice cautious" and make it quite clear from the start that marriage is not on the schedule.

It may be that divorced men with children have the biggest hang-ups. Several weeks ago my friend Joseph called to ask if I would meet him and his nineteen-year-old son for a drink. I wanted to work that night, but he made a special request, so I agreed to join him. He had come out to New Jersey to straighten out a family problem that his ex-wife was frantic about. Their seventeen-year-old daughter had been cutting classes and staying out late, and Dad was summoned to lay down the law.

Joseph established a curfew and spread around some strong talk. Afterward, in the bar, he analyzed the problem as being his wife's fault: "She doesn't relate to Peggy;

she doesn't project any feminine ideals for Peg to look up to."

The son, Steven, agreed. Obviously he was impressed at being old enough to share his father's confidences, to sit in a bar and have a beer. Obviously, I came off as the cool and perfect mother, with her children under control, just exuding "communication" and "femininity." Joseph thinks I'm brave, noble, with it, the ideal mother. That's really flattering, but it gave me a bad turn to get these kudos over another woman's strained, if not broken, back.

Divorced men can be very harsh when talking about their ex-wives and all the things they do wrong with the children. I'm sure a good bit of this is a defense mechanism in action; they feel guilty because they aren't around to shoulder the day-by-day responsibilities of the kids. They are only there on weekends or whatever their visitation arrangements are. Some divorced men dislike divorced women. There they are with the house, the kids, $10,000 or $20,000 a year in alimony and tax-free child support. Oh, the bitches!

Well, it's unsettling, confusing, and rather eerie to be placed in a never-never land as a widowed mother who is nobly carrying on, doing everything perfectly. To some divorced men, any problems I have with my children are simply because they don't have a father . . . but any problems they have with *their* children are usually blamed smack on the ex-wife. It's hard for them to see that some of the run-ins with my kids are my own damn fault . . . just as a good many of their children's major and minor delinquencies would have occurred whether or not they had a father in residence.

Jessica told me about a man she loved and could have married, but he told her it was impossible: "If I can't raise my own kids full-time, it would kill me to have to bring up another man's children." He was not talking about finances, either, but the twenty-four-hour role as a father to two young boys. "What bothers Ted most of all is the fact that he sought the divorce, knowing that he would have to relinquish his position as a real father and become one of the part-time variety."

Blind Dates

Remember how nervous you were years ago when your college roommate or the gal next to you in the typing pool offered to "fix you up" with a date? And you said yes, and she did, and it turned out fairly well. (A surprising number of widows and wives meet their husbands on blind dates.) It was important to have "dates," to be popular, to go out. More significant, however, is the point that way back then the blind dates were drawn from a pretty regulated, "safe" circle. If you were at school you were meeting other students, and hopefully you had interests, goals, and courses in common. If you were at work, your matchmaker would of course try to pair you with someone who liked short, blond girls, if you were short and blond, or tall, dark girls who played chess, if you were tall, dark, and played chess.

But now the mix is not so easily obtained. Well-meaning friends, for example, will pair you with *any* single man they know—whether he be gay, widowed, divorced, a woman-hater, or a combination of those—who happens to like short, blond girls. Perversely, you are tall, dark and like to play chess; you have three children and he hates children, and on and on and on. As Marjorie, a divorced friend, explained when I wailed about my unfortunate blind dates, "It's not like college, Rae, when everything was circumscribed and you were meeting guys in a very controlled situation. Now you may meet a plumber whom you respond to physically but not mentally, or a lawyer who you dig mentally but not physically, or a long-term bachelor who in no way is going to get seriously involved."

While Karen has met most of her dates through friends,

Marilyn observes that this "only goes on for a certain length of time. I think it comes down to one blind date per couple. And because people are trying, you want to be nice, but eventually I got through this blind-date period and started to make contacts on my own, which is really the best answer."

"Blind dates supplied by friends don't continue after a few months," says Fran. "Hostesses may feel they have to find a date for you so that they can have a nice even number at dinner. But when it becomes a bother to dig up a single man, it's often easier not to invite you."

Blind dates are still a part of our social scene, but moan and groan all you will, they are often a better answer than more up-dated approaches of mixing. Don't expect or rely on handouts from your other single friends. Single women of any stripe are notorious hoarders of eligible men; it is only when a friend considers that a man is of no possible use to her that she will pass him on to *you*. Sometimes these hand-me-downs can be valuable, but don't hold your breath waiting.

Gloria, who was widowed a few years ago, told me her story. "I had become friendly with a girl who was divorced for a few years and seemed to have a lot of dates. We would go to the movies during the week, but on weekends she was usually busy. When I hinted that maybe some of her dates had some friends and we could double, she became a little cool. Charitably though, a few weeks later, she called to tell me that one of her beaux was unsuitable for her—that's what she said, 'unsuitable'—but maybe I would like him.

"It turned out that this man was a widower with two mixed-up children, and although he was perfectly nice, my friend would never consider marrying him: if she was going to have problem children, she wanted them to be her own. A fair enough statement. Lee passed him on to me, and he turned out to be a marvelous person I enjoyed talking to and going out with."

There are more contemporary versions of the blind date: computer dating, commercial matchmakers, video-dating services, and the increased use of personal classified ads. The goal with these approaches is the same as that of ordinary blind dates: to turn compatible strangers into friends. The difference is that with the old-fashioned variety, a friend or acquaintance introduces you; here the medium is a computer, a questionnaire, a videotape presentation, or the pick-and-choose flexibility of placing or answering provocative advertisements.

Computer Dating

This first form of electronic matchmaking enjoyed a vogue in the sixties, when, not surprisingly, the computer was coming into its own as an adept servant in many areas. There are always enterprising geniuses who are quick to seize a new gimmick which may satisfy particular needs of vulnerable humans. (This is after all how one young man made three million dollars in three months before Christmas last year when he "bred" the proliferative species named "pet rocks," the answer for many lonely people who didn't want messy pets.)

In any case, while the father of computer matchmaking has remained more or less anonymous, his services have been widely publicized. For quite a few years, numbers of lonely men and women would pay $25 to $50 to a money-making entrepreneur, who would use a computer to match their personal needs, desires, income, appearance, goals, education, and the like with those of another. It seemed like a good idea, but the results didn't live up to the promise. For one thing, most people find it hard to define themselves via the medium of short-answer questionnaires which are then used as the basis for the computer log. Often their real dreams and idiosyncracies remain buried in a way that no form survey can plumb.

Also, although the deeds which can be performed by computers are indeed wondrous, they are still machines and not people. As any *Star Trek* fan knows, you still need Captain Kirk, Mr. Spock, and Scotty to operate a star-ship. And you need people to match up other people. Often the owners of the computer-dating systems were computer operators and businessmen with no background whatsoever in psychology or human relations. And, in addition, there was little personal interviewing. Basically, after your data was fed to the computer, you would receive a list of people whom you should call, or who would call you. Usually you were guaranteed ten or twelve calls per month, but often there weren't enough similar files for the computer to draw on, and the list would dwindle down to two or one—or none.

Of the almost one hundred widows I interviewed, only one admitted to having tried this type of dating, and she asked me not to use any name, not even a pseudonym. "I paid fifty dollars for a three-month membership. The first month two men called me, but we didn't hit it off in either case; the second month, they gave me two numbers to call myself and said that four men would be calling me.

"One call I made was to a widower fifteen years older than I who told me right off the bat that he had turned over all his assets to his grown children. I didn't care about that at all—I'm not looking for a rich man—but I did care that he chose to establish this 'ground rule' immediately. The second man I called sounded nice until he suggested we meet and go dutch to dinner. Again, I can pay my own way, but I didn't like the cold, 'window-shopping approach,' so I turned him down.

"Of the four who were supposed to call, only two did, and one of them sounded ashamed of the whole idea, which made me feel embarrassed. I did agree to meet the other man (although I was frightened at the idea), and while we had a pleasant enough evening, there was no future. He was much too intellectual for me. My idea of a nice time is to go bowling or to a movie; his was to stay home and read a good book. And then too, neither of us in any way met the physical requirements we had set up. We were both disappointed, and there was no point in meeting again.

"The final month, there were no numbers, which, of course, convinced me to write the whole thing off as a rather bad experiment."

The New Match-Makers

The second generation computer-dating services don't even mention the reliance on the marvelous machine, but you know it's there. Now the emphasis is on "the professional project director," the one person who will see that you get "individualized service of a superior type," as described by the "Central Registry Matching Service," a New York/New Jersey organization. You don't pay fees for match-making—you pay membership dues, about seventy-five dollars a year.

Central Registry guarantees "at least ten matches . . . the average person gets thirty to thirty-five matches in one year . . . Hundreds of marriages mean that we are doing something right." The questionnaire/application form is extensive and could give a true picture of the applicant as well as the type of person she wants to be matched to. The problem again is whether or not most of us can or want to pigeon-hole our personalities with such check-off surveys.

For example, question twenty-five reads:

Personal Physical Appearance is considered by others as

_____ exceptionally good looking
_____ pretty or handsome
_____ attractive
_____ average
_____ less than average

Would anyone answer "less than average," or by the same token, "exceptionally good looking"? I recently read an interview in which William Holden described his looks as "very average," an opinion I don't share. But whether through modesty or what we view as the truth, we simply do not see ourselves the same way that others see us. The question and its answer are not only meaningless but misleading.

> I most desire
>
> _____ prestige
> _____ knowledge
> _____ power
> _____ wealth
> _____ security

The one word answer I would have to fill in on such a survey isn't even included: happiness.

Then there is the most ridiculous pair of questions I've ever seen on a "social" survey:

> Are you now or have you ever been addicted to drugs?
>
> _____ YES   _____ NO
>
> Have you ever been convicted of a felony?
>
> _____ YES   _____ NO

I would guess that every single applicant answers *no* to these questions as well as one about addiction to alcohol and whether or not you were ever confined to a "hospital for the treatment of mental illness."

This particular group has been in business for eight years, so (in their words) they must be doing something right . . . or at least their advertising brings in enough new hopefuls who are willing to pay seventy-seven dollars a year for the chance of meeting at least ten new dates. At $7.70 a date, it's not a bad price; you would spend easily that much at any singles club . . . or during any given evening at a singles bar.

Video-Dating

It might be more worthwhile, however, to spend your money on this latest innovation in matchmaking. Groups such as Video-Mate and Video-Date (see Appendix VI) use the same basic questionnaires to sort out compatible ages, backgrounds, educational levels, hobbies, and other interests. Then a short TV tape is made of an interview between you and a staff member that provides some indication of your personality and, of course, your appearance, in a way no computer could. Your tape is then shown to male subscribers who seem to be in your dream-man category, and if they like what they see, you look at their tapes. Finally, if you like what you see, full names, addresses, and phone numbers are provided.

At New York City's "Video-Mate," 600 clients pay $125 for three months of service, and they can renew their memberships every three months at half that cost. So far it seems to have been more successful for women in their twenties and thirties than for those who have seen forty. Marlene Scher, an executive director of the company, says, "Women over forty are often left out, because the men their age come in and ask to date younger women, and we can't do anything about that."

In St. Louis, a fairly new TV dating service, View-A-Date (see Appendix VI), has sent more than 100 people out on matches in less than five months. Connie Majkut, the attractive founder of the company, reports that her clients range in age from 18 to 65, and "most of them seem to have been very well pleased." She charges fifty dollars for a three-month membership. A four or five minute TV interview is taped, and each month a member is allowed to view three different tapes.

I checked out a group called "Video-Date" in Maplewood, New Jersey, which describes itself as the original TV dating service (in fact they recently won a suit against Video-Mate for copyright infringement). The director, Stan Subarsky, and his assistant, Grace Paredes, both have training in social work and are warm, intelligent, and sensitive people, as well as single. Video-Date is about a year old and has five hundred members; their new Georgetown franchise in two months alone has enlisted one hundred members.

As Grace explained, "Our clients have priorities; they aren't losers. They know themselves and don't want to waste time, money, and effort on partying to find someone who may turn out to be just a body for Saturday night. They are looking for in-depth relationships, not the superficial ones which are all too common with the bar scene."

The tapes were the best proof of her point. Pretending that I was a client, she ran off three tapes of men in their forties whom I might be interested in meeting. The impact of seeing someone "alive" on the screen, talking about himself honestly and openly, in conversation with Grace (Stan usually does the interviews with women), is impressive. Fred, 47, for example, is a very handsome man, divorced with three children, interested in movies, theater, books, who says, "I want to spend time with a basically nice person who has good values and could enjoy some of the things I enjoy. Mass participation does not interest me."

Another man, Paul, 48, had a marvelous sense of humor which would not show up on any questionnaire. Although the TV picture made a liar out of him, he described himself as made of "pure, solid fat but I'm trying to change this." He said the most desirable trait in a woman for him was a "sense of humor and mutual interest, mutual understanding." He noted that he's very flexible and "can tolerate an awful lot in a person before I get upset," and he admitted to being "selfish, hedonistic, and capable of being a little crazy—doing my own thing." Paul would expect a date to be totally honest and not hide behind any pretensions.

But you see the mere reporting of these tapes cannot give the same impression as actually *viewing* them. I then looked at two interviews of widows in their forties who were attractive, knowledgeable, and interesting . . . but would have fared badly at other forms of singles socializing. This was an ideal way for them to get their personality and appearance and goals across in a comfortable and significant way.

Stan did a five-minute taped interview with me—it was relaxed, easy, and pleasant. When I watched a replay, I was happy with my image; a prospective date could get a fairly good idea of what I'm like as well as how I look. I liked the whole approach. I especially liked two of the three men whose tapes I had seen; if I had the $125 for a three-month membership, I would have joined. Unfortunately, I'll never know the answer to the question, Would Fred and Paul have liked me?

The Personal Classified Ads

All my life I've been an inveterate reader of classified ads. I read automobile ads, employment ads, antiques ads, and the personals, and most of the time I'm not looking for a car, a job, or an antique. In the past year, though, I've been paying attention to the personal section, which in my local paper, for some reason, always precedes the automobile ads. Here is where you'll find the legal notices saying that Smith, J., is no longer responsible for the debts of Smith, A., and here is where you'll find tickets available for the next Bowie concert, along with the dubious, "Your child can be a TV model," and the honest, "Organic gardeners—manure for your garden. Will deliver." You will also find what used to be called

"The Lonelyhearts Ads." (In fact, Aunt Rose, although at a very with-it 65, regards all self-motivated singles attempts as simply different forms of lonelyhearts clubs.)

Actually, the ads are honest attempts by lonely people to meet understanding and likeable people of the opposite sex (Some ads are interested in the same sex, but that is not our concern here.):

Professional Gentleman —45 yrs. 6'1" independent, wishes to meet professional female. 30-45 yrs. Call ——— 3 PM til? Ben.

Athletic 6/2 50ish bachelor, loves finer things, well traveled, seeks attractive-funlov'g lady, coll grad pref. Box ———.

SUCCESSFUL
prof'l gentleman, just turned 40, relocating in this area. Loves tennis, bridge, skiing. Anxious to meet fun loving, attractive young lady to share mutual interests, Box — ——.

These were from my local paper, *The Bergen Record*. I also read *The Village Voice*, which has three or four pages of personals every week, including:

ENGLISH MILLIONAIRE
looking for girl to share the joys and sorrows of life. Must regard money as secondary. Box ——— .

FASCINATING
WIDOWER:
6' 170 pounds in great shape and loves golf. Wants to meet a truly exciting/exceptionally attractive woman who laughs easily. Box ———.

I am educated, brite, divorced, sensitive (to both other people and myself), musing, responsible, attrac, creative, sane, successful, brave, clean and reverend, 46 going on 38, interested in meeting brite women w/style, taste, gd looks (not nec. beautiful) who is serious but not solemn, likes to laugh but is not silly & who has no hangups but is not kinky. This reads like the mating of a prince & princess but what it really says is I'm looking for a gal w/my vibes. Send cards & letters now as offer is limited. Box— ———.

Answering classified ads is a very hard thing to do, and most of my research group of widows wouldn't do it. But, I convinced myself that if I read *The Village Voice* and *The Bergen Record*, and I'm a nice person, albeit lonely, there must be some nice people out there, too. I answered all the ads reprinted above. I worked hard at coming up with clever responses, but in all my replies I mentioned the fact that I was a widow.

I received an answer from one ad, the second gentleman, who seemed like a nice enough divorced man with grown-up children who would make a good date—for someone else. To be honest, I really didn't like his photograph, and on that level alone, I didn't respond. I should add that, not being a complete dummy, I rented a box at my local post office so I would not have to reveal my true name and address.

When I received no answers from the other ads, I decided to conduct a little controlled study. I typed answers to the ads on another typewriter and said I was a thirtyish divorcee and did not mention my three children. A friend with a business box in another town allowed me to use his number. And I received interested responses from *all* of them. I did not follow up, because the message was clear. These men were: a) looking for younger women than I and b) regarded divorcees as more likely dates than widows or at least were not frightened off by divorcees.

I still maintain that there are some nice people who place such ads and nice people who answer them. If you choose this approach (either placing or answering), I stress caution and truth—you may never get a letter in your post-office box, but for $10.00 a year, at least you won't run the risk of being hassled by either a professional sex-racket operation (which, I have been informed, some of these personal ads represent), or a less than stable person who may complicate your life. Basically, you're not taking much more of a chance than you would if you talked to a strange man in a bar . . . and decided he was nice. At least the anonymous post-office box gives you a chance to choose and think about it before acting.

There is competition in the advertising field. A fairly new magazine, *Singles World*, is filled with ads by men and women of all ages, and all single types. All the ads sound very honest and straightforward, but I was a bit dismayed to see that ads placed by women outnumber those placed by men by more than ten to one.

On balance I think it's worth a shot, as evidenced by that very nice man who did write to me suggesting that December 3 (his birthday) and July 21 (my birthday) could be an interesting match. "Why not try a call, and who knows but that a vodka martini might even be followed by dinner and champagne."

Singles Bars

If you are twenty-five, look like Sally Struthers, and have been accustomed to going to these "meat markets" before you were ever married, you will have no problem making the scene now. If you're ten or fifteen years older, however, have never been to a bar alone or with a girl friend, and are both emotionally and intellectually timid about the idea, you will *hate* singles bars. And in a way you should, because there is one common factor about all singles bars—the women are looking to get married and the men are looking to score. I don't say this in a self-pitying kind of way. It is simply a fact of seventies life.

One psychologist, who is divorced, and has been to a few singles bars in his time, disagrees with me strongly. He said, "Have you any idea how many *women* go to singles bars to get laid, to enjoy the one night stand? I'd like to meet some attractive, possible women too, but I never find them in the singles clubs. Still, there are some that are worth going to, and who knows, someday, I might meet the exception."

Cathy, who had been married for fifteen years to her high school steady, said to herself, "What the hell, I've got to do this—everyone else is, and it's better than sitting home all alone." She collected some references about singles groups and one night decided that the bar action with a well-publicized college graduates only, 30-to-45 age limit, bar/club was better than her church rap group, and plunged into the scene.

She reacted: "What bothered me most is that the very thing I thought I would escape by being with a 'congenial, single group' was even more apparent than it would be if any single or married woman or man walked into any swinging bar on their own. Sorting out the creeps from what I thought were the good guys (bad value judgment at best), I then spent the next two hours with two very presentable gentlemen who eventually confessed that they were married!"

Anita frankly admitted she "just couldn't handle the bar scene. I'm a very talkative, gregarious person, but this is not for me. I did not, I cannot, and if it means I'll never go out again, I probably still would not go to one of those places, although I have divorced friends who often do and have a good time."

Millie also expresses this attitude. "My bringing up has probably hurt me because I over-react, and sometimes I let opportunities go by because my parents wouldn't have liked me to do it—even though I'll never see forty-five again. Some of my friends go to bars and have a grand time, but I can't."

Lorraine has a slightly different reason, although her background figures in her decision, too. "I would never go to a singles bar. For one thing, I just can't take in that much liquid. I couldn't sit for hours doing nothing but drinking."

Marilyn admitted she has never been to a singles bar. "A few nights ago a few friends and I decided we must be going to the wrong places. We don't meet any fascinating new men—they all seem to be people we already know."

Irene went to one singles bar and "it was godawful. I would never join singles or widows clubs, although whatever works for someone is fine. I tend to believe the sort of person who would join is not my cup of tea."

A Chicago psychologist who would rather remain anonymous, and is also a bachelor, comments, "Everybody talks about how awful singles bars are, but when the alternative is to stay home, it's better to go. It's not unnatural to have the feeling that you don't want to expose yourself, but it isn't natural or comfortable, either, to feel alone, unnoticed, unwanted. Many widows and divorcees feel they'd rather take that feeling of being in a 'meat market,' as you put it, than to sit at home and do nothing."

A more objective view of what the singles bar scene is like was reported by Jesse, a barman at Maxwell's Plum, which is one of New York's most popular singles hangouts. Jesse told *New York Magazine* ("The Action at Maxwell's Plum," June 16, 1975), "I remember a night a guy gave a chick a hundred dollars to streak. She disrobed and bolted around the bar like a bunny in heat. This is an 'in' place. You got to expect that sort of thing. The chicks in here don't wear bobby sox and chew bubble gum, y'know. They're *sophisticated.* A lot of guys have come in here whacked out of their heads, man. I mean buzzed. A lot of guys come in here who have their wives stashed somewhere else. Yeah, we get a lot of lonelies.
. . .

"It's always the same. Monday, you get the out-of-towners; Tuesday, the women who come in after the theater or the cinema; Wednesday, the regulars, the New Yorkers; Thursday, the businessmen, the divorcees, and the wives looking for a little extracurricular activity, though they have to catch the ten o'clock train home to Long Island; and Fridays and Saturdays, the B.B.Q.'s."

(In Jesse's lexicon, this last group stands for singles from Brooklyn, the Bronx, and Queens.)

It's not clear from his breakdown which night is Widow's Night, but for this widow, the only time I'm comfortable at Maxwell's Plum is lunchtime, when there are no swingers of any category in sight!

In an article on singles in the *New York Times*, Susan Jacoby wrote, "Whatever their age, sex, economic status, or location, singles must contend with an image problem which frequently combines the old picture of the lonely loser with the new, excessively carefree stereotype. The special image of singles affects both their personal and professional lives."

Over the past year, I have ventured into more than one singles bar alone for reasons that go beyond conducting research. I cannot report that these forays were easy. You hope for a seat at the bar, because if you're forced to stand, the going is that much more difficult. You will be pushed aside and elbowed by "serious" drinkers, women in pairs or trios, people more vociferous, taller, and more at ease than you are.

Once you sit down and order your drink, you will leave the change of your five-dollar bill on the bar, to prove that you are there to have a congenial drink, that you are not waiting for someone to *buy* you a drink. Also, the bartender will be friendlier because he feels he will get a tip, something which many women, unused to this action, forget to leave. And then you wait.

I have sat in bars (five or six) and memorized all the labels on the bottles behind the bar, figuring that this would make me look intelligent, and besides it gave me something to do while I was waiting. I have sat in bars and pretended not to have any matches so that I could ask the man next to me for a light, thereby generating conversation as well as fire.

I have realized that a woman sitting at a bar by herself is actually a sitting duck, not to mention a dead pigeon. A man can maneuver around a bar, going at will from one pigeon (or duck) to another and take his pick. A woman at a bar has to pray that the man who lights her cigarette or voluntarily talks to her will be nice, because if he's not, she only has two choices: stick with him or leave. If she leaves, that either means going home or braving another bar.

Although my own survey could not be considered in-depth, I have met some very presentable men in singles bars in and around New York and on vacations. Nothing much ever came from these encounters.

Doris, on the other hand, is still hanging in there. At a Little League baseball game last week she told me, "I went to the Bicycle Club the other night because I couldn't stand staying home again. I met a man five or six years younger—I'd actually met him before—and this time I gave him my phone number. Really, I'd rather go out and have dinner with him than listen to my divorced friends moan and groan about their wretched exhusbands."

JoAnne hasn't made up her mind about singles bars one way or another. "I went to a very fancy place with a friend of mine, and it was nice to have two guys come over almost immediately and offer to buy us a drink, but Linda's 'date' was wearing a wedding band, and mine was so evasive about his situation that I had to assume he was married. So that outing was a bummer as far as I'm concerned."

A week or so later, she gave it another try at an "ordinary" restaurant where she and her husband Jack had had dinner occasionally. "I found I was much more comfortable on my own. I talked to the bartender—who wanted to date me—and I did meet a divorced man who I saw a couple of times afterwards. I don't know, it's not a nice, easy way of meeting people, but it beats staying home all the time."

The recent hoopla about *Looking for Mr. Goodbar*, the

bestselling novel by Judith Rossner, is not too encouraging, either. In this book, the heroine meets a man in a
bar, goes home with him, and is murdered. When the TV
ad for the paperback edition ran—at 7:00 in the evening, I
must add, when I was watching TV with my kids—it
soured me on any men I might meet through this approach. It seemed as if this prime-time programming
could signal last-time encounters for lonely women trying
to meet someone special.

And it led me to the conclusion that, with few excep-
tions, the only way you can make the bar scene, or *should*
make the bar scene, is if you are accepted as a long-time
"client" and friend, especially by the other regulars, and
are not regarded therefore as someone on the make. But
this kind of action is difficult for widows with young children, or for those who don't like to drink, or don't have a
"neighborhood" bar in the immediate vicinity, or must
simply be home, zonked out, trying to acquire enough
energy for the next hair-raising day.

Singles Clubs, Groups, and Other Alternatives

If the idea of meeting men in a bar is an absolute turn-
off, there are other singles-oriented activities that could
prove more attractive. Unfortunately, discovering the
right organizations requires trial-and-error searching and
solid determination to make new friends.

For Kate, such clubs are out of the question. "Actually,
I'm probably a snob about it all, and I get the impression
that going puts you in a 'for-sale' situation. But most of
all, I'm too shy to join groups of any kind."

Although she has never joined a singles club, Pat feels
"they are seeking a happiness they'll never find. Happiness must come from one's inner self, not from material
things or people."

Eve did join one group before she remarried. "I wasn't
too interested, but I felt you never knew when you might

meet someone special, and I took advantage of every opportunity." Incidentally, she did not meet her new husband through the club; they were introduced at a party given by mutual friends.

Most of the widows interviewed were really not aware of the wide scope of formal and informal groups, special interest organizations, church-endorsed rap sessions, newsletters, directories, and profitable businesses designed to get singles together.

Catholic, Protestant, and Jewish authorities, recognizing the growing population of unmarried men and women, and a concurrent widespread distaste for singles bars, have launched or sponsored many of the most successful activities. Some groups are mainly social, others are cultural, some are "therapeutic" in the sense of talking out mutual problems, and others combine all these functions.

Olga is in her mid-forties with a sixteen-year-old daughter. "I'm not about to go to bars or singles dances." But she's found an outlet for loneliness through her church, the Ecumenical Singles Congregation of Bergen County, New Jersey (see Appendix II), which provides an alternative to regular churches, "where everybody seems to be paired off," or the singles scene. "We talk, we socialize, we plan dinner and theater trips, and we're all very comfortable because everybody is single," she says.

"Single Again" is the name of the group which meets every Wednesday evening at the Universalist Church in Manhattan. On an average night, about 175 men and women, all wearing name tags, pay $3.00 for an hour of socializing before splitting into smaller discussion groups. At the end of the discussions, there's another social hour. Designed for "the formerly married of mid-years," Single Again has a good rate of return visits: about 60 percent show up every Wednesday night. The group is run by a steering committee which directs the events and selects topics for discussion as well as oversees the training of discussion leaders.

Most of the formerly marrieds who attend are not members of the Universalist Church and a good percentage are not even Protestants. They come from all sections of New York City and its suburbs.

A similar situation prevails at "The City Singles of Marble Collegiate Church," which meets on Tuesday nights for dinner, talk, and social activities. The age level is from 35 to 50, and the average attendance is about 100. One of the members stressed that what was nicest about City Singles is "I belong—there's warmth and love and concern here." Most social evenings end with dancing to records of big bands, but recently, the club had a Hustle Night, with a professional instructor. A spin-off of the original City Singles meets on Thursday nights for similar activities and is limited to those who are 21 to 35.

The First Unitarian Church in Brooklyn Heights is the scene for a less formal, more intimate singles club which meets on Friday nights in the church basement. The members are mostly in their thirties, and activities range from discussion groups to charades, but the emphasis is on congenial talk, helped along by wine or beer. Again, most of the participants are not church members, but the church provides the location, and any money left over from the $3.00 admission fee after expenses goes to the church.

A closer tie between singles and the religious sponsor exists at the Brotherhood Synagogue on Gramercy Park in New York, which avoids "the formality of a very structured rap," according to Ernest Glogover, president of the steering committee. "We prefer to be a neighborhood drop-in kind of situation," said another member of the group, who noted that most members live fairly near the synagogue.

Actually, of all the religious/singles projects, it seems

to be the Jews who are most concerned about the growing singles population and who offer the most activities on a nationwide level. Any moderate-sized synagogue will have at least one club or special activity for its unmarried congregation, and it is generally open to outsiders as well. In my part of Bergen County, which is definitely suburban, there are at least four or five events held each week at any of three area synagogues, ranging from wine and cheese tasting parties to more serious lectures and discussions.

Over two years ago, the Federation of Jewish Philanthropies recognized the need to provide an alternative to singles bars and formed a Task Force on Jewish Singles. Aside from ongoing studies, the task force publishes a newsletter which now has a circulation of 2,000 and distributes a booklet describing coffee houses, sabbath dinners, discussion groups, and other current programs. At a recent conference in New York, Rabbi Eugene Sack noted that in Manhattan alone there are perhaps 100,000 Jewish singles who had either been divorced or had avoided the early marriage traditional in the Jewish faith. After analyzing various singles activities Rabbi Sack reported that large mixers were characterized by "ruthless competition"; a better choice is "smaller groups whose members meet regularly and develop loyalties to each other." At this writing, the task force had organized programs in thirty synagogues in New York, Boston, Chicago, and Los Angeles to take Jewish singles out of the bars and bring them back into the synagogues.

Another religious/singles group with branches all over the country is COPO—Catholic One Person Organization (see Appendix II). I first heard about COPO at a dinner party when a friend told me her widowed sister had met a wonderful man at a meeting and that they had subsequently married. My only reservation about this marvelous match was that the sister had four children and the husband had eight, a blown-up Brady Bunch to be sure.

But Louise reported that the kids were pleased about their new siblings, and especially happy to have two parents again. So you see, if you try hard enough, there might be a happy ending after all.

I have tried very hard for the last year, but I have not quite found my singles niche yet. My first adventure took me to a meeting of Parents Without Partners in my area. I did not enjoy it, perhaps because the group was too heterogeneous. It is not so much that I too, like Kate, am probably a snob, but more to the point, I had little in common with the people there, either mentally or socially. Most of the women were divorced and quite bitter about their exhusbands, problems with the children, and so on. And the men were uncomfortable with my identity as a widow and my profession as a writer.

However, it was a first step. As the psychologists say, "Action beats inaction any time." Action also leads to reaction. Another widow I interviewed went to a Parents Without Partners meeting, and although the eligible men were not her type at all, she met three other women (one widowed, two divorced) with whom she had a lot in common. They all became friends and established a small but solid corps that enabled them to brave other singles situations together.

The next singles trip I took was to join a club called The Party Vine (see Appendix VI), which publishes a monthly newsletter listing about sixty different singles events for "college-type" people. To join, you must fill out an application giving your educational background and pay an $18.00 annual membership fee. I complied (although I was cynical about the check on my college degree) and waited eagerly for my first newsletter. It was crammed with a rich assortment of social goodies: from political meetings to charitable benefits. It seemed like a good way of controlling the selection of people I would meet.

That first month I went to a meeting of "The Citizens Group to Draft Ted Kennedy." It was held in an unused cavern of a room at a bar on Fifty-seventh street in New York. The only connection the "meeting" had to Ted Kennedy was to charge an admission fee of $5.00, presumably to be spent on ads, flyers, and the like for this lost cause. Drinks were two dollars each; there were a few half-empty bowls of peanuts on the bar, over-loud, frenetic rock music which made most attempts at conversation impossible, and a rather interesting assortment of people. It was not very different from a singles bar.

But having bought myself a drink I thought I might as well enjoy it. I declined several offers to dance and spent some time observing one 35-ish man who was vigorously taking down phone numbers. He would talk to a girl for about three or four minutes, get her number, and move on to the next conquest. When he got around to me I commented on his style. It turned out that Rusty was from California and would be in New York for just a week. In about half an hour he had booked himself solid with dates!

I finally maneuvered myself next to an attractive man whom I thought I'd like to talk to and had just opened my mouth when I was literally pushed aside and almost bowled over by a suitcase-sized handbag, propelled by a very determined lady. She succeeded in cornering what had been my prey, and I decided the whole thing wasn't worth another two-dollar rum and tonic.

A few weeks later I tried another event which promised better possibilities—a "Non-Joiners" cocktail party. I liked the sound of that, and the organization was described glowingly in my newsletter. "This club is seven years old and never advertises. Over 600 people attend because the Non-Joiners serves as a screening ground for the prestigious Edwardian Club, which is mostly professional and executive." The party was held at the Rainbow

Grill in New York's RCA building, a lovely spot I'd always enjoyed, and it was scheduled for a Sunday night, which was promising too, because it eliminated the married men who are usually home with the wife and kiddies on Sundays.

I went up to the sixty-fourth floor filled with pleasant anticipation, which died as soon as I got off the elevator. I cannot describe the party as anything less than a mob scene. I was quickly hustled out of my $5.00 admission fee and given an invitation to the Edwardian Club's next outing—"we don't give them to everyone you know" —but I noticed the ticket-taker gave them to the next three people behind me in line as well. Again, two dollars for a rum and tonic. And then the "promenade" began. There were so many people that if you stood still, you would have been trampled, so I moved and moved, as restlessly as the other 599 of us. In one room, people were dancing and the crowd around the floor kept circulating, on the lookout for connections, contacts.

Some people were successful and would move on together, at least for a while. Several men wanted to talk to me, but they weren't appealing, and I employed the old bit from college-mixer days and would not make eye contact. It wasn't worth it. After thirty minutes of this (during which I made the promenade twice, pausing only to look at the marvelous view of New York), I thought, "Look you paid to get in here—try to make the best of it. Talk to someone." I stopped walking for a minute and spotted a nice looking man dressed rather strangely in a mint-green corduroy suit and orange suede boots. As I walked toward him, I noticed he had a jade elephant on a chain around his neck.

"Where did you get the elephant? I've always wanted one." Not a bad opening. "Oh, this little thing. I picked it up in Israel last year." There was a definite lisp. He was gay. However, having gotten this far, it seemed only polite to make small talk. When I asked why he was here, he pointed to a rather chubby lady and said he had promised to escort his sister. "I would never come to these things," he said. "There are no attractive men here." Of course, he was talking about his own chances, but it was definitely true. There were no attractive men for either of us!

I told him he was absolutely right, put down my drink, got my coat, and drove back home to New Jersey, just in time for the last installment of *Upstairs, Downstairs.* I had been gone exactly one hour and twenty minutes and had spent only thirty-five minutes with the Non-Joiners. The name was apt. At least *I* wouldn't join them again.

However, two swallows don't make a summer . . . and two parties can't possibly tell the whole story. My Party Vine newsletter lists meetings of the Young Jewish Singles of New York, the Hellenic University Club, a Chinese Cooking Demonstration, a French speaking cocktail party and game night, the New York Ethical Culture Society, the Catholic Alumni Club, a tennis group every Saturday night, a meeting of the New Democratic Club, a party given by the Young Republicans, and the twice-monthly cheese and wine meetings hosted by Party Vine.

I think if I had the time and the energy—and the money—I could find a group that would be congenial for me. And I will certainly try again because we're surrounded by "do-gooders" who want to make money while making singles happy. For example, another organized singles activity called "Dinner Parties Unlimited" ($18.00 annual membership), is for gourmets and gourmands who like to eat in different restaurants (see Appendix VI). These joiners also go *en masse* to concerts, Broadway shows, lectures, bus trips, and nightclubs, and the club promises "best of all—good companionship and intelligent conversation."

Another commercial enterprise I checked into describes

itself as "the nation's largest and fastest growing 'life-style' organization." Insight Dynamics Corporation was established in California in 1967 and claims over 12,000 members. More sociologically or psychologically oriented than other singles clubs, their "social concept" is for singles to meet on a one-to-one basis. They offer group activities, diversified programs, travel plans, and "intrapersonal growth." Membership in Insight Dynamics costs from $65.00 to $150.00 a year depending on how much growth you're looking for.

The core of this group, which now has headquarters on both coasts, is called the "IDC Experience," a twelve-hour seminar which in structure and content is not unlike the widely publicized est meetings. In fact, the founding father of Insight Dynamics, twenty-nine-year-old John Raymond, could very easily fill in for Werner Ehrhard himself. A high school drop-out at 16, a powerhouse lecturer by 18 in 1967, at age 20 in 1969 Raymond came up with this new twist on help for singles. The seminars, many of which he personally conducts, will help you "see life as an alive, exciting experience . . . achieve new higher levels of consciousness and awareness . . . discover new technology for pinpointing and solving problems . . . and increase your income and 'abundant living.' "

You begin with the "Experience" and then move on in terms of your needs and checkbook. My checkbook was balking, so I couldn't experience the entire experience. But psychologically, too, I'm not one to be spurred on by "The Power of Positive Thinking" programs, but for widows who could use some mental shoring-up, this might be a solution.

Most of the profit-making groups also offer travel plans at reduced fares and attractive packages for singles. Party Vine, for example, highlights several different tours each month; one especially intriguing possibility was a trip to Bali, Hong Kong, and Manila—two weeks for

$995.00. However, there was that old "single supplement" that Bea Green talked about in chapter seven that added $100 to the cost.

Travel and vacations are a good way of meeting men while you see the world, provided you have the money. One of the most publicized singles travel plans is Club Mediteranee which has Sybaritic hideaways all over the world.

Janet tried a Club Mediteranee jaunt in Martinique. "While I wasn't quite prepared to go topless, as everybody else seemed to be doing, I met a neat doctor from Cleveland who was just as embarrassed about the whole ambiance as I was. No, I didn't end up marrying him and living happily ever after, but we shared a good vacation together, and later, back in Cleveland, he took me to a few parties and I met some more people."

Last year I considered the Club Med in Martinique but was gently discouraged by my friends Doris and Lee who had been there a few years before. I like to take my kids with me on vacations, but aside from the topless bit, Doris and Lee said there wouldn't be much for them to do, and the crowd might be a little too young for me. At the family-oriented Club Med in Guadaloupe, there are families, not singles, so there wouldn't be much for *me* to do. Ultimately, looking over the brochures and reading their enthusiastic promotional literature, I decided that this kind of programmed love-in was not my bag. I do not want to be hugged and kissed by a handsome, but unknown, Club Med staffer—the initial contact one has upon arrival. Nor am I interested in one or two weeks of hedonistic, pleasurable but very temporary living-it-up and loving-it-up in a tropical paradise, which all Club Meds seem to be. I would rather take my chances for long-range contacts in a less exotic setting.

I ultimately did go to Martinique (but not to Club Med), where I had a marvelously enriching vacation and met some nice people. When I pay off this trip by next February, I'll look for another island and keep on trying.

Some women can't bear traveling alone or with their children, but this is a joy for Tina who has been doing this for the last nine years. "I enjoy it and can cope with any problems. But I have a friend who just got divorced—her third one—and she literally cannot make an airplane reservation by herself. She must get married again." We both wished her luck.

Fran has been widowed for more than a decade, and she says she would never go on a vacation with another woman. "Aside from the problems about where to go and what to wear and all that nonsense, if I'm with a woman, other groups of vacationers, including married couples, don't ask us to join them. But if I'm alone, I'm included in groups, and often this means some single men will be around, too."

Taking the Bull by the Horns

If you're simply not meeting any worthwhile men, and you find that some of your new friends are in the same boat, take a tip from a group of New York City widows, divorcees, and unmarried ladies: form a club of about a dozen women and once a month, hold a party at one member's house. Each member contributes $10.00 which covers the cost of food, spirits, and cleaning up; the person hostessing the party pays nothing. Each woman is asked to invite two men, if she can. This is a good opportunity to include some men you may not be interested in personally, but who someone else may appreciate.

Carla, who has been widowed since 1965, is taking a slightly different tack. She has started an informal club composed of single and married people of all ages who find they would like to have brunch or supper and dancing on Sundays in New York City. "We will keep the costs down to about ten or fifteen dollars a person, and it will be a congenial atmosphere and a good mix of people who could turn what is often a dull day into something enjoyable for everyone."

Now that you've heard about how, and where, and even when to meet men, there are considerations about going out with them that should be reported.

Rules, Regulations, and Practicalities About Dating

Don't treat new boyfriends like your husband. Maybe you've had five or ten or twenty years of catering to a man, which was nice for your husband/wife life. But this is a new life. You can make a man nervous or edgy if you're constantly asking him what he'd like for dinner or which movie he would like to see. On the other hand, if you have a nice relationship going and your man seems to like coddling, then go right ahead and fetch-and-carry if this pleases both of you.

This bothers some widows, however, who feel that a newly single man, whether widowed or divorced, is too eager to make an immediate transference to another wife. Lorraine said, "I try not to get in a groove of cooking meals for a date, or to make him feel too much at home. I'm not his former wife and I don't want to be treated as if I am, not unless I'm seriously interested; and after eight years as a widow, I've never been seriously interested."

Don't continue to see men you dislike just because you don't want to hurt their feelings, or you think you may meet others through him. The former attitude is masochistic and the latter is unrealistic. Some of the more together single women I've talked to agree that men have their own rules about women: if there's no future in it after the second date, they drop her. Often this means no sexual future. It's time women followed the same set of rules. If you haven't had a really nice time with a man, don't continue your, and ultimately his, suffering. You can be more lonely on a boring date than you can be at home doing something you enjoy or watching your favorite TV show.

Anita doesn't mind telling a man he doesn't appeal to her or that he doesn't attract her. "It's the only way. But I've been a widow fifteen years now, and I never would have been so honest years ago." Marian thinks it's only a question of being fair. "If a person doesn't seem to be my type after one or two dates, I don't continue seeing him. Why hurt someone unnecessarily or be bored unnecessarily?"

Karen feels, however, that if friends have gone through the trouble of arranging a blind date, she owes something to them and the date. "I would go out with a man and try very hard to be interesting and interested, and at least see the man one more time. But this backfires because then somebody boring may keep calling you, and I just don't have the heart to say 'I don't want to see you.' But I found if I said no often enough, he would finally get the idea."

Another reason to be selective and weed out the wheat from the chaff is that time is precious. I try to work at least four nights a week and spend the other three nights with the children. Of those four nights, maybe one night I'm too tired or turned off to write. This leaves three. If I have one dinner date, my productive night-time work— my best time—is cut by a third.

I'm too old to waste time going out to dinner just so I can say I have a date. I did that twenty years ago. I'd rather stay home with my kids and get down to my office by nine instead of wasting time on a so-so engagement. Not only does it take up the evening, but I have to spend some time preparing for the date, and then the next day, I'm so tired I can't give the right effort to *that* day's work. If someone is special, interesting, exciting, then fine —I reserve my dates for those people. I've been staying home a lot lately.

Marilyn agrees. "In the early years of widowhood, I enjoyed going out more than I do now. Now I'm often more comfortable or happier if I stay home and read or do my needlepoint." For Amy, the answer is not so simple. "Socially, you're darned if you do and darned if you don't. Sometimes you can get just as depressed going out as you are if you're home alone."

I have always believed in personal research, and for this book, of course, I was motivated both professionally and socially. Here is my record of social achievements for the first year, starting about six months after Alex died. I offer it more as a realistic assessment of the possibilities than as an up-beat success story:

> **Blind Dates:** 6, including an especially awkward one arranged by my father; follow-up dates: 3
>
> **Bars:** 15; dates resulting from these adventures: 8 (one married); follow-up dates: 4 (with one man).
>
> **Parents Without Partners:** 0
>
> **Party Vine Parties:** attended 3 different events; met half a dozen phone-number-takers, but none I would go out with.
>
> **Classified Ads:** 0; six letters answered: 1 response; 6 phone calls made: 2 too young, 2 didn't like me, 2 I didn't respond to.
>
> **Parties** *(given by single friends):* 3; met 3 men: one I'm sure could be certified crazy, the second was a nice widower looking for a nice mother to take care of his nice young children, the third I've seen two more times for dinner.
>
> **Vacations:** 3 *(fairly successful):* met men on the beach, in a few bars (see above), and at a gambling casino.

> **Other:** professional meetings (4 or 5): 2 new
> men; follow-up dates: 7 (with one of these
> men, who unfortunately was married).
> **Meaningful Relationships to Date:** 1, which
> lasted two months.

The singles scene is enriching, but defeating, uncomfortable but honest, frustrating but challenging. If you
keep with it, and you must, you will eventually meet some
interesting, if not promising, men. Some will be married
(and you'll have to cope with that moral problem), some
will be divorced and never want to tie the knot again, and
some will be widowed, like you. Some may have much in
common with you, and some will be confirmed misogy-
nists who will skitter and run at the very implication of a
"permanent thing." You, personally, will have to make
some decisions about "one-night-stands," holding out for
another wedding ring, or something in between. In any
case, you will have to learn to deal with sex—having it,
enjoying it, scheduling it, getting along without it—which
is discussed in the next chapter.

9 *What Is This Thing Called Sex?*

"For months I felt as if I were dead from the neck down—and sometimes dead from the neck up, too. But when I finally had sex for the first time since my husband died, I felt alive again. And I cried, and I told the guy 'thank you,' which I'm sure he didn't even understand."

This statement from Gloria, a forty-six-year-old widow, is typical of the way many of us react to their first sexual adventure after the death of a husband. The thank you, stated or thought, is for bringing us back to life; the tears are a final goodbye to the husband you will never sleep with again.

However, the first experience is not always totally satisfying as Suzanne, a Los Angeles widow, told me: "My first affair was a nightmare. I really wanted to go to bed with my friend. We had a good relationship going head-

169

to-head. Physically I was very ready, and I thought I was emotionally, too. But I started to cry at the most crucial time, and absolutely ruined the moment. Fortunately, my guy was understanding. We tried again a few days later, and it was good, really good. In my mind, all those months I had turned off any memories about sex, but it was so great to finally recapture this part of my life."

The first time out is the most traumatic. As Dr. Richard Conroy, Director of Community Psychiatry at St. Luke's Hospital in New York City states, "Widows have difficulty reaching out without the presence of a man. They are locked into the mores of our society. They feel they are considered 'fair game' by men. They also have tremendously ambiguous feelings about having an affair. They might be intrigued by the idea, but then they don't enjoy it."

The last statement may be too much of a generalization. Some enjoy it, some don't, and some won't even participate. Most of the widows over sixty that I talked to, whether or not they had been recently widowed, declared they would not consider a sexual relationship with a man unless they were to remarry. Further, they flatly admit that their sex drive has diminished.

Interestingly, some of the widows in their forties also have widowed mothers and find that a definite generation gap exists in their sexual habits, even though they now share the same status. Marilyn said, "Mother has had quite a few offers to go to bed, but she simply wouldn't even think about it." Jessica observed that her widowed mother "is very content with her state, and she feels that that part of her life is over and she can certainly do without it."

Then there is a group of widows in their fifties, for whom the idea of sex is intriguing and the need for sex is recognized, who wouldn't dream of an extramarital affair. After the death of her first husband, when Lorraine was dating the man who would be her second husband, they did not go to bed together but conducted a "perfectly proper" year-and-a-half courtship. "We just hadn't been brought up that way, and we waited until we were married. I don't even know why we behaved so strictly, but we did. Although I feel somewhat different about it now, I still wouldn't go to bed with a man unless I was really in love with him. And I haven't met someone I could feel that way about."

Recently *New York* magazine (January 26, 1976) reported in a comprehensive article, "The Sexual Diamond: Facing the Facts of the Human Sexual Life Cycles," about the progression and tapering off of one's sex drive. The thrust of the report was that women in their forties are at the peak of their sexual needs and most able to respond "creatively." Further on in the article, author Gail Sheehy (who adapted the piece from her book *Passages: Predictable Crises of Adult Life)* notes: "After forty, as the aging process sets in, vaginal lubrication will diminish to a degree. But it need not impair a woman's pleasure or receptivity. Sexologists offer a very direct piece of advice: use it or lose it. Indeed, it is the woman who continues to engage in an active sexual life, even without hormone replacement, who shows the least evidence of this physical change."

Sheehy points out that some women can compensate for the estrogen loss resulting from age by drawing on estrogen produced by the adrenal glands. "They age well, remain strong and energetic, and enjoy much the same vaginal lubrication and elasticity they have had all along. Although this defense against sexual aging is out of a woman's control, the other most important counteractive factor cited by Masters and Johnson is not. And that is regular intercourse, once or twice a week over a period of years."

This is a hang-up for millions of younger widows. Physically we need sex—to keep our hormones in balance as well as to achieve the satisfaction and gratification that can only come from sex. Mentally, we feel we are too young to spend the rest of our lives without it. But we lack partners.

As JoAnne says, "I needed sex immediately. Even though I was in mourning and as depressed as I was, I felt the need for sex, but I was without it for a year and a half, which is unbelievable. I didn't masturbate for the longest time until I was finally climbing the walls. My analyst told me I should because I would be less dependent on a man. But truthfully, that's what made me feel *worse* about it, because it underlined the fact that there wasn't a man around."

Only 20 percent of the widows I surveyed relied on self-help when there was no husband or lover on the scene. Yet, statistics from a recent survey place the number of all women who masturbate at close to 80 percent. It may be that many of us are as turned off from *any* sex by the lack of a male, as JoAnne was.

Because sex still involves a two-some in the eyes of most widows, some may turn to other women for sexual pleasure. According to *Redbook Magazine's* survey of more than 100,000 women, "(Those) in the separated-divorced-widowed group were the most likely to have sexual experiences with other women." Ten out of one hundred single women reported such experiences compared to four out of one hundred married women.

For widows who want to resume heterosexual activities, consideration of when and how this reintroduction should occur is not as important as realizing that this is the beginning of a whole new orientation to sex. Because of "The Sexual Revolution," more and more people go to bed with more and more partners. But you are older and have hopefully become accustomed to a fairly steady diet of sex that you like and need. You may have become less resistant to the idea of going to bed with "other men" than you would have in those long ago days when you were *really* single.

In analyzing the *Redbook* survey, the magazine's editors reported: "When we looked more closely at the sex lives of women who are separated, divorced, or widowed, we found that they tend to be more sexually assertive than married women in general. They are more likely to initiate intercourse, for example, and be active partners."

At least fifteen widows told me that their sex drives had increased since their husbands died. In two cases, this heightened appetite was seen as a release from former sexual problems. Three women felt that the lack of regular sex made it seem that much more desirable, but, significantly, ten thought the increased drive was related to their own new perception of themselves, coupled with straight-out physical needs. "You have to shake off this idea that it's fine for men to fool around but somehow 'sinful' for women. Where would men be without us?" remarked Virginia. "After all, it works both ways."

There was an element of practicality, too, in some of the discussions about what used to be called "free love." As Mary-Anne, who has been a widow for five years, said, "You wouldn't marry someone at this point in your life without sleeping with him first, would you?"

Vera, however, was not so up-key. "I think the lowest blow to a widow is society's assumption that she cannot get along without sex. It leaves her the prey of every would-be Lothario. We became widows, not animals. Being a widow does not give a person a permission slip for promiscuity. If she is raising children, she can hardly teach them morality while she is practicing immorality. What any widow is really seeking is a lasting relationship like the one she lost."

There are other practical aspects about these revised attitudes on sex that most widows face.

The Right Motivation

It's important not to use sex for the wrong reasons: the big bed is so empty, or it's part of the new vogue. Having intercourse with a man, or a series of men, should be a personal, selective decision based on physical and emotional needs. If you're only *taking* from your partner of the moment or *using* him, it won't be very satisfying sex, anyway.

Joyce Brothers says, "Some widows go from man to man to man. This won't solve anything. There is a tendency when one is left without sex to either overdo it or else close it out. Don't be pressured into either approach. Don't become a monk or an indiscriminate swinger. You have to make a judicious choice and do what you think you should do, not what you think other women are doing, or what your old rules dictated you should do."

Irene had her first sexual experience three months after Peter died and in five years has had about seven affairs, some one-nighters and several long-lasting. The first time she felt "sad, guilty, remorseful and good. It was a release and sensual. All I knew was that I enjoyed it but didn't want it to go on. It was like a parenthesis in time, a way to get back to myself. This first act wasn't important, but the memory was. I still wanted to mourn."

Terry's experience was in direct contrast to Irene's. "The first guy I went out with was a nice man and all, but I didn't have any feeling about going to bed with him. The second man was a widower, and we spent the whole night crying about our mutual loss, and maybe this kind of sharing meant more, but we did not have a physical relationship. For at least a year after I started dating I didn't meet anybody I felt that way about. Not that I had a moral thing about this, but I think I really didn't meet anyone attractive enough."

Although Terry personally didn't find this so strange,

she said, "Friends of mine can't believe that men are willing to go out with me if I won't go to bed with them, but I've had several relationships like this which lasted a long time and never ended up in bed."

Fran's husband was ill for two years, and during the time he was in the hospital, she had a long-lasting affair with a doctor. "We knew it was a relationship that wouldn't go anywhere, but it filled a definite need for companionship and physical contact. Although I had been at the hospital every day for months, I had never noticed this doctor who had been there all the time. And he walked over and invited me to dinner, and we immediately began a relationship. It had nothing whatsoever to do with my marriage, even if Jerry had survived. It was just what was necessary and satisfying to fill a need."

Fran explained in more detail: "Sex has never been lacking in my life, although when I was married to my husband, I never thought of being unfaithful to him. I loved him so much, the idea of sex with someone else never even entered my head. But in this case it filled a void—as it turned out, for both me and my doctor."

The turning point for so many widows is realizing that you don't have to be head over heels in love with a man to go to bed with him. "Love, of course, is ideal," said Janet, "but about two years after my husband died, it finally occurred to me that I was depriving myself of pleasant, even enriching, experiences by waiting for that Knight on a White Horse. Since then, although I haven't had that many affairs, the ones I've had have been satisfying and worth it, and I didn't suffer from that much guilt, at least after the first time."

Where, When, How

Logistics are sticky here. There are three alternatives: your place, his place, a hotel or motel for the night. If you have no young children, you have no problems. Your place, of course, is ideal. I'm always amused when I read *Cosmopolitan's* articles about successful sex in your own charming apartment. There are never any young creatures in the background (except, perhaps, for a seductive cat); you always have fragrant flowers and lovely, fresh sheets in the bedroom, the right brandy, the most inspiring nightgown, the perfect little breakfast, and *The New York Times* for the morning after.

When my first sexual encounter occurred, the house was a mess and the sheets were due to be changed when my once-a-week miracle worker came the next day. There was no brandy, much less the *right* brandy, and three little beings were very much in evidence, sleeping like angels in the next room. Although the sex itself was somewhat revivifying, I spent a sleepless night (in a less than inspiring nightgown—not one of my priorities during that stage of widowhood) praying there would be no thunderstorms to send Robbie scurrying to my room for solace. I finally booted my friend out of bed around 4:00 A.M., ushering him to the safety of my workroom, which also doubles as a guest room.

After getting the children off to school the next morning, I woke my guest with a friendly glass of orange juice, made some coffee, and offered him toast or cereal as the perfect "little" breakfast, then selfishly hogged the front section of the *Times*. A bad habit to be sure, but I'm hooked on the *Times* and not used to sharing it these days.

Subsequently, I a) put a simple hook-lock on the bedroom door, b) tried to teach the children that Mommy is entitled to privacy, c) always pray that there is no thunderstorm on a particular night, and d) bought some inspiring nightgowns.

The nightgowns and I remain fairly virginal, because after several more casual contacts, it became clear to me that sexual revolution or no, I was still attached to the old-fashioned notion of love. Thomas Merton, the well-known Trappist monk, had an incisive view of sexual love despite his celibacy: "The act . . . should by its very nature be joyous, unconstrained, alive, leisurely, inventive, and full of a special delight which the lovers have learned by their experience to create for one another."

In my life as a widow, I've felt this kind of experience with only one man, and it had to end. Since then gut-level needs have taken over a few more times. Now, on the rare occasions when a man stays over, I don't sneak him out of the house while the children are at school. I still insist that he spends the remainder of the night in the guest room, and if the kids are home, we all have a good breakfast together. My friends are their friends. And I'm even a little more generous about sharing the *Times*.

While I do worry about what the children think, especially at this stage where relationships are fairly transient, I do not worry about what the neighbors think if they see a strange car has been parked overnight—and they *will* think the worst! If you're thinking about what they might be thinking of you, then you really don't want a man to stay overnight. Worry about what you think of yourself.

Beth is comfortable about her position and knows her children are still too young to understand. "But I always ask them for my privacy and demand it and get it. I manage my sex life very carefully, with closed doors."

JoAnne also doesn't care about her neighbors, but does worry about her children. "I always insist that a man removes himself from my room before morning. But the first time I brought a date home, it was really awful. We got there about 11:30, and my nine-year-old daughter was waiting up. She started to cry about the fact that I had gone out with somebody else. 'You're married already,' she told me. 'I don't want you to get married again.' Obviously that was not an easy night for Ben or me."

Those widows who have had sexual experiences agree that your place is better than his place unless you can arrange to stay overnight. One widow told me about her standing arrangement with a sleep-in sitter every Wednesday night who can take care of her children the next morning. This may remove some spontaneity to sexual plans, but it also removes confusion and the horror—yes horror—of having sex, bumbling out of bed, climbing into your now-wrinkled clothes, combing your hair, and making the sad, silent trip home.

If you live in a city and your man is at all gallant, at least he will take you home in a cab, although the trip will be grumpy, heavy, and both of you will be wondering, "Is this really worth it?" But if you've *driven* to meet your date—often the case when suburban widows date urban bachelors—you may have to make the drive home alone, one of the most wretched situations ever encountered. Then it's not worth it.

As for motels, going away for a weekend with a man can be delightfully romantic and pleasing. But if you're meeting in a temporary room for the night, or a few hours, because his place is out and your place is out, it does become rather shabby and depersonalized, as anonymous as the room itself. Janet said, "Making love in a motel is plastic-wrapped—like the glasses and the toilet seat and the soap bars."

Controlled Affairs

Possibly as important as the where-when-how is the *what* to use for birth control. Men automatically assume today that most women are on the Pill. This is a very arrogant assumption. To begin with, why would a nice, "decent" widow still be taking birth control pills? Aside from the fact that sex is not a daily occurrence in her life unless she's into an enduring relationship, by now she may be worried about the consequences of years of taking the Pill.

My gynecologist told me some time ago, after my first son was born, "Birth control pills are for single girls who rely on impromptu sex and the romance of the situation." In other words, for an old married lady like me, a diaphragm was safe, easy to use, and to hell with the spontaneity. His recommendations have been endorsed more recently by doctors across the country whose reports, published almost monthly in every leading women's magazine, stack up to the diaphragm, and the condom, as the safest, most effective birth control methods currently available.

It would be ridiculous and chancy to take birth control pills in anticipation of sexual events which may never take place. Yet at this point in my widowed life, I could definitely do with some spontaneity. I've been meaning to talk to my doctor about the new morning-after pills.

Despite your personal choice, the prevailing attitude now is, as it certainly was years ago, not to depend on the man to establish control. It wasn't really funny, but I had to laugh when Cara-Sue, an Atlanta widow, told me in her charming southern accent about one romantic evening that had progressed to the bedroom. "Ah told my man this wasn't the right time of the month for me, and he said, 'Darlin', don't worry about a thing. I have a very low sperm count!' "

True Love or What Passes for It in the Meantime

There are instances when love is here to stay—for the duration, maybe forever, but definitely on a day-by-day basis. How does one handle a long-term affair, a lasting relationship, without the benefit of a title, a ring?

For some women this is easy, natural, and absolutely right. The other night I called a friend in Milwaukee. Her number had been changed, and when I dialed the new number, a man answered the phone. When Gerry got on I asked, "For God's sake, are you married?" She wasn't, but she was as happy as a clam. The kids were ecstatic about Bill; she was schoolgirlish in love and enthusiastically redecorating her new home; and if I sent them a Christmas card, I should address it to Mrs. L and Mr. B!

Another widowed friend has lived with her man for four years, a fact accepted by her college-aged daughters (who do not live at home) and her twelve-year-old daughter who does. Actually, Tanya and her man would like to get married, but Jack simply doesn't earn enough money to support a family of five, and if they were to marry, Tanya would lose all her Social Security benefits, about $200 a month net.

In five years as a widow, Kate has had one long-range relationship and no other dates. "But it was a good relationship. I felt like a school-girl again and found the sex very satisfying. When we finally talked about my husband, he told me he thought I was very 'noble.' It was romantic and exhilarating, but I felt his interest level waning, and I broke it off rather than being dropped. I couldn't chance that."

Beth has lived with two men since her husband died four years ago. She's been with her current love for a year, and they are planning to get married. "I never consider the children's school teachers or my neighbors a problem. The question is: 'Do I want to continue to live in a non-married state?' And the answer is 'no.' I believe in marriage and I want to commit myself to that."

Other women have drastically changed their attitudes about the idea of living with someone. Martha, now 54, feels that despite her social upbringing and background, "It's not really necessary today to get married, and if it would cause great confusion in finances, I would simply live with a man if I loved him. I wouldn't bat an eyelash about it."

Linda, 47, says, "I'm not a prude at all. If you want to do something crazy, I'm right with you, I've really changed a lot. But I've found you have to be so careful.

Men will take it the wrong way. I'd have to be convinced a man wouldn't think less of me for letting him live with me without being married."

Several younger widows felt the living-in wasn't really necessary. Karen, 43, said she wouldn't have someone move in unless she married him. "This is a personal viewpoint, but I don't see where actual residence is called for. My husband spent a lot of time here before we were married—dinner, weekends—so although we didn't really live together, we knew what it was like to spend more or less normal time together. I would definitely want to have that kind of experience with anyone I was interested in, but I don't necessarily want to announce to the entire neighborhood that I'm living with a man."

Marilyn has had three close relationships in the ten years she's been widowed, but "we didn't in fact live together. I never thought living with someone was my bag, but now I feel that marriage isn't really necessary. If I met someone I loved and it was right, we would live together."

I personally don't think I could do it, but as one date said to me the other night (the same man who originally said I inhibited him), "If you fall in love and the relationship is meaningful, you'll find a way of dealing with your kids, your family, the P.T.A., and those neighbors. But if love isn't there, there's no sense even thinking about it."

Playing House on a Short or Long-Term Basis

There are other variations on this sexual theme that are important, and generally, it's not the duration or the twenty-four-hour-a-day nature of an affair that matters; it is what the alliance represents for the widow.

Jessica, for example has known someone very intimately for three years. "Because this relationship hasn't culminated in marriage, gradually it deteriorated, and I think we're about to end it. There was nowhere to go with it, and even the physical aspects have disappeared at this point."

Ellen frankly admits to playing house for two years, although she and her man did not live together. "He fixes things, the way my husband used to, and plays with the kids, but he's not available emotionally, and so therefore he's a phantom, really not at all like my husband." The psychological explanation of this is that Ellen is re-enacting her husband's "rejection" or desertion of her. She couldn't be angry with him for disappointing her by dying, so she found a man she could be angry with in reality.

Gina was not angry so much as amused. "When I met Charlie, I didn't compare him to Ed, but he turned out to be so much alike. After we married, the differences were funny, though, because Charlie assumed I could fix plugs and do mechanical things around the house as *his* wife had, and I assumed *he* would do these things as Ed had. Fortunately, we found a good handyman who saved both of us."

Sexual problems, not electric toasters, were Lorraine's difficulties the second time around. "Although I enjoyed sex and it was fine, it was not as good as it had been with my first husband. After all, we knew each other so long, and I liked the way he made love to me. But I didn't see how I could tell my new husband that he was doing something wrong, or that he should try something else."

Eve found that the comparisons that made her nervous were those produced by the grown-up children of her second husband. "Of course they remembered their Mom, and here I was, stepping into her place. Every time I moved a piece of furniture or cooked a family dinner, I was worried that they would compare me to Lee. This went on for about a year or so, and then I realized that they were nice kids and happy their father was happy, and that they accepted me for myself, not as a replacement for their mother."

Some widows are frightened about any enduring relationship, because the idea of losing a man—either to death, disinterest, or, perish the thought, another woman —would be too devastating. JoAnne recounts her experience with a "wonderfully attractive man. In fact, he looked so much like my late husband, it was scary. When he came to the house, I found myself deferring to him for decisions I ordinarily would have made. For example, what would be the proper way for my daughter to answer the phone when she babysat while Murray and I went out for dinner? I was playing a role of coparent or wife, instead of the single-parent role I'm forced to play normally."

When she and Murray split, JoAnne went through a mini-version of the grief she felt when her husband died. "But it was not as catastrophic, even though I was afraid it would be. I don't know. Maybe I didn't really love him, or maybe you just get hardened to accepting your losses."

In my own case, when a special friend found he had to straighten out his life alone before we could build a life together, to my amazement I didn't fall apart, and except for one bad night and the next day, when I drank too much, and played sloppy, sentimental songs for hours (badly) on the piano, I then continued with my life. I know I loved this man and could have had a happy life with him, but I think my experience mourning for Alex amounted to an unconscious type of learning about self-protection, or self-defense if you will. In a way I built a little wall around myself so that I couldn't be hurt by this loss.

When you're a widow, you become more philosophical about sex and at the same time more realistic about it. Fran admits that as she approaches 60, her sex drive is diminishing. "I mean I don't have an affair every day, or every week, or even every month. I am a little calmer about it now, although when I was first widowed at fifty, I was almost hedonistic for several years in my search for physical gratification."

The big clinker, as always, is love, and my friend Nancy summed it up most effectively for all of us. She said, "Sex with a stranger is so different from sex with someone you love. It's escape kind of touching. Not that it can't be good, but it's rather like having a sandwich when you're starving for a feast."

Part 3

I AM I PLUS MY CIRCUMSTANCES

10 | *Acceptance of I-Me-Mine— New Dimensions*

Spanish philosopher José Ortega y Gasset once wrote, in a work on the nature of man's personality, "I am I plus my circumstances."

I first read that years ago in college, and the concept has always stayed with me. *I am I plus my circumstances.* A beautifully simple equation that sums it all up. The I and the circumstances change, and that is what any phase of life is all about, whether adolescence or widowhood.

As we have seen, during widowhood your circumstances and your I will change. Initially, you do very little thinking about yourself—your thoughts are directed to your husband, to the changes in your not *solo* but *married* life. Finally, though, you enter the period statisticians call "recovery," as early as three months after your husband's death or as late as two or three (or more) years afterward.

187

At this point you have learned to let go of the past and are beginning to build a new life. For most of us the stressful time is over, and, as LIMRA found, "There is a reintegration in terms of the widow's new situation with her past adjustment. She develops a new set of functioning roles. And once again, she is oriented to past, present and future." There is not much in-depth data on this particular stage because once adjusted, widows fall back even more into the woodwork. "Most of the literature," according to LIMRA's study, "is about the widows who do *not* make an adjustment."

Recovery. What a marvelously rich word. What a cryptic way of describing and condensing all the events that have lead to adjustment. But it's apt, no denying it, and there will be some blessed day when you realize you have "recovered." You are able to accept the new you and your circumstances. You are no longer just functioning or surviving—you are living!

For Irene, the recovery state did not emerge until well after two years. "I would say more like three. Even though I acted in plays, produced plays, integrated myself into a good segment of the local society and arts, I did not want a working relationship with a man. I kept a good distance. I actually began to enjoy my independence, lonely or not. Always during those first three years I thought no one was up to Peter, and I was right. I compared every man I met to him. Only in the last two years can I say that the comparison was valid but dead, because he is dead. I want new comparisons and a new life; new thoughts with new people. I want more for me and of me and from me than I had or was five years ago."

Mary Martin recently discussed her own widowhood and subsequent recovery with Eugenia Shepherd. After her husband, Richard Halliday, died three years ago, she ran—to Europe, Brazil, Palm Springs, New York. She tried to escape because, as she says, "I was completely helpless, but now I'm learning to walk by myself." She describes her life as a series of circles. "I've been sad for a long time, and I'll never get over missing Richard, but I feel that I'm starting a new circle." As part of the new circle, she is selling the ranch where she and her husband had been so happy and reviewing the possibilities of stage appearances, which will help her and please her vast audience.

Barbara has remarried, but she hasn't forgotten her roughest times as a widow and her survival. "You see, at that time you think your problem is the only important one, that your grief is the only grief there is in the world. But the truth is you do get over it. That old cliché is still true: time does heal all wounds."

The real recovery stage hasn't been reached by Kate yet, after five years. "I'm aware I have to get to that point, and this awareness makes me feel I'll make it. I'm certainly working at it."

Marriage, Maybe

Most widows recognize the fact that the odds on remarrying are not in their favor. The figures are 7 in 100, and for widows aged 50, the chances are only about 20 in 100. If you're younger, the odds increase slightly in your favor. Men are more likely to remarry than women because their potential wives usually cover an age span of twenty years, from young women right up to their own age level. Women are usually limited by the few available men in their own age brackets or older.

By now you should be trying to live with these statistics. Keep on trying. Try for meaningful relationships, which have to be more important than wearing a wedding band or finding a father for your children.

There was a sharp age break apparent in the survey of widows who did or did not want to get married again. Those in their sixties had no major urge to remarry, and, like Pat, "doubt that I would find another husband as good as the one I had." Widows under 60 still have hope but are realistic:

KAREN: "I guess I assume I will get married again, but if I don't, I don't."

DEIRDRE: "I'd love to get married again, but I'm not too optimistic about it. Actually, after Ian died, I thought if I ever got married again, it would be either for great money or great love, and there's no reason to get married otherwise. So far, there's no reason."

MARY-ANNE: "It's amazing to me that I haven't remarried. My first proposal came three weeks after my husband died. But now, after five years, I think everyone has given up on me. The offers don't come as frequently."

JEANNE: "As for marriage, now I want companionship, someone I can enjoy, someone I can depend on."

HELEN: "The hardest thing I really haven't come to terms with yet is that there can't really be a replacement."

ANITA: "I want to marry again, but I'm so frightened of marrying someone who may die. Although I know you can't predict what's going to happen, I go out of my way to avoid what might be another death."

Therapist Martin Sylvester feels that, for many widows, getting remarried is still a main goal when the major attitude should be adapting to single life. "The push for a substitute husband, a replacement, is really detrimental and leads to disillusionment and unhappiness. When a person relaxes, when she's not looking for a husband but simply looking for a good life, she is more receptive and desirable . . . and her chances are much improved for actually finding someone special."

Fay is no psychologist, but she is one of the wisest ladies I know. She's been widowed for many years, and at 74 still supplements her Social Security by babysitting. She gave me almost the same advice as Martin: "If you are stimulated to other things, sometimes your dreams will come to you. You have to create something for your-self, and often that will start a chain of good experiences for you."

Learning to Be Selfish

In the best sense of the word, this means learning to talk about yourself and your likes, dislikes, goals, needs. You are in the recovery state when you start doing what pleases you, eating what pleases you, wearing what pleases you—when you stop thinking in terms of what pleased your husband. That was one part of your life, yes, and a good part. But before you met and married him, wasn't there an individual who had her own thoughts, tastes, moods?

You know you're on the way to making it on your own, as your own woman, when you stop saying we and start saying I. This doesn't mean you must never mention your husband again. It only means that you say, "*I've* always liked Frank Sinatra," or "*I've* always wanted to go to Japan."

"I had a very delayed mourning process," says Kate. "I think I finally recovered when I started counseling after five years. I coped by working working working and not thinking about myself. I'm now trying to think about *me.*"

Suzanne feels that her husband's death forced her to start living for herself. "After years of feeling that I got pleasure only through others, my husband, and child, I have to come to grips with what do I want to do with *my* life. I'm still struggling with that one; some days I get closer, some days I feel I'll never get nearer to a solu-tion."

Alice is more optimistic. "I'm on the verge of a new life with a new man, and I'm doing things I want to do. My career identity as a writer has taken a backseat during these last bad years, but now my hope is to pursue it once again in the near future."

For some widows, however, the we is always more comfortable, and, like it or not, pops up at the oddest times. Marilyn says, "After ten years I still say we, and people don't even know who I'm talking about. I think it will always be like that."

Seeking and Finding Help

Now you're no longer banging your head against a wall or calling friends in the wee, small, and depressing hours of the morning. Maybe by now you don't need to talk it out; you can manage without help. But if you need help, at this point you could be involved with widow's rap groups or other mind-expanding directions, and, just possibly, helping someone else in turn.

Some of the most significant self-help or mutual-help programs have been established by widows themselves. Gerontologist Virginia Van Coevering describes her own state after her husband died as the "gelatin syndrome" or confusion and the general inability to function normally. This eventually led her to pursue a doctoral study of widowhood. She wrote, "Like the sharing of mutual problems encouraged among drinkers through A.A. or among the overweight through Weight Watchers, the coming together of widows for discussion can help them adjust to what is recognized as one of the most difficult changes in their lives."

Joyce is helping other widows make it by becoming a minister. She's in her third year of divinity school and made the decision because "I was so angry at the ineptness of the clergy. Most clergymen take care of the funeral and then shuffle off the bereaved to someone else."

Aunt Rose would advise widows to "give lots of love to the children and never lose faith. Ask and pray for guidance. Yes, we shed many tears, but He answers and helps some way, somehow."

Lorraine has also tried to help widowed friends. "I listen to them, try to make them see that it will get better, that they will start to live again, even though both times it happened to me there was nobody who came forward to help me through the bad days."

Irene was helped by psychiatric counseling. She joined a gestalt group two years after Peter died and then saw the leader privately for about a year. In terms of helping others, she says, "Yes, I could be very supportive, let her go through her periods of recovery, and urge her to take her time." I can personally vouch for her supportiveness. Ironically, I didn't know how to deal with her husband's death—he was so young; the children were babies; she was making a major move from one coast to the other.

All I could do or say at the time was that I was sorry. But when Alex died, Irene called me from California and offered truly constructive sympathy, if there is such a thing, and a very empathetic ear, and our conversation was heartening and helpful. Now when I talk to widows, I feel, of course, that I can offer the same understanding. Someone used to say when telling a lame joke, "You had to be there." We widows have been there!

You Like Yourself . . . And the World Seems Brighter

It's a psychological truth that if you are pleased with yourself, other people will respond with pleasure. You have to develop a new persona, and, happily, most people eventually do after personal tragedies. They do survive, not simply because they have been strong enough to hang on by the fingernails but also because the I-Me-Mine concept has taken over, and you say, "Dammit, I'm okay. I'm a good, attractive, smart person."

Here is what some widows say and think of themselves:

JANET: "I was so smug before. I had a solid marriage, beautiful children, everything. So when you weather something like this, you really come out of it as a much more aware person; maybe that's why we widows seem to relate to each other so well—not just because we can compare notes on how horrible, but we've really had to shake up our lives. My daughter's reaction was that this tragedy, her father's death, can only happen to other people, it can't happen to me, but we widows have worked through the fact that it did really happen to us!"

TINA: "If you like yourself, other people will like you. That's a psychological truth. I went to a party recently that I had doubts about; the guests weren't my type of people at all—society types—and this made me nervous. I didn't feel as if I looked my best; I was nervous, overly shy, and had an awful time. The hostess, however, kindly asked me to another party a few weeks later, and I was up and had a wonderful time."

GLORIA: "As bad as I felt, I wouldn't leave the house unless my hair was just so and my make-up was on. It was a point of pride. You don't want people to say 'look what a mess she's in since her husband died.' You try to compose yourself. When Jeff died, even though I was prepared, it was hard. I would swallow and swallow and say to myself 'try, try, try.' And I tell this to other widows at wakes. You can't stop trying."

LINDA: "I often wonder how I was able to do what I did do, because I never had this image of myself as that strong a person. But now I think I'm more aware, more able to function as a person than friends who have been married for years. They take so much for granted."

EVE: "For some women, widowhood is the best thing that ever happened to them. Psychologically, they finally emerge and become their own person, while maybe they were in the background all their married life."

KAREN: "I definitely think this whole debacle has made me a better person. For one thing, I don't let little things bother me as much. They don't seem as important. I used to blow up about so many insignificant things. But now I'm calmer; I have a better balance of what's important and what isn't. And also, I can't stand to see friction between married people . . . not even a fight, but just being unkind to each other, or holding a grudge. It really upsets me when this goes on. I do tell them, too, that they should consider how lucky they are to be together and not squabble about such silly things."

CAROLE: "This was the strongest experience I've ever been through. Nobody helps you. Even your best friends."

JOANNE: "You change what were your former hang-ups. When I was a girl, I went seriously only with Jewish guys, because I felt this was something I owed by parents. Now I date whomever I please; I don't owe anybody anything. I paid my debt and married a Jew. Ironically, other people change too. Now, when my mother found out I was with someone not Jewish, it didn't matter, and it didn't bother her that I might be having an affair with someone and not marrying him. She just wanted me to be happy."

Eleanor, 53, told *Time* magazine, in the special issue on women: "When Bill died I was a gloved, girdled and hatted upper-middle-class mama. There was no need to work, but I could not tolerate sitting in that house being the 'widow of . . .' or the 'mother of . . .'. What it finally came down to was the whole thing of being a person. I wanted to make it on my own." Today, after being a widow for seven years, Eleanor lives on a houseboat (instead of her former suburban home), and works full time helping men and women in a program called "Investigation Into Identity," in Rochester, Michigan.

Some Prices You Pay

Your new independence and sense of self-identity can not be bought without paying some taxes in return, however. Although Lorraine jokes with her lawyer about this now, she still remembers the day, right after her second husband died, when she went to her lawyer's office on business and started to cry. "I told him, 'You'll have to excuse me, I know I'm going to cry.' " She got control of herself and then went on to discuss her financial affairs. "Now, he laughs about how independent I am, and is always after me because I don't let him open doors or hang up my coat.

"Actually, he's being complimentary, but at some point, he told me seriously that I was too independent, that I managed everything so well, that maybe this puts men off. But I'm used to taking care of myself now."

As Janet said, "There must be something to becoming more self-sufficient that maybe discourages men who would like a more dependent woman. Maybe because of this I don't recognize the opportunities that there are."

One date told me that I was becoming "tough," and although I think he meant that in a good sense, it made me sad. I think there is a point where you become so used to surviving that in a way you cannot accept outside help. I'm not there yet, and I don't want to reach that point. I want to retain my identity, and, if you like, my needs as a woman.

Ironically, however, the fact that you are functioning quite well, thank you, is a hang-up for some men. Recently at a dinner party I got into a near-argument with a man who pompously said that he was working to leave his wife enough money—several hundreds of thousands of dollars—so she would never have to work or worry about putting the children through college. When I tried to explain that there was more to widowhood than financial comfort, he didn't understand what I was talking about and accused me of being a "women's libber," hung up with "penis envy." His wife smiled approvingly and spent most of the discussion examining her manicure.

People live in a dream world, and widows have some special insight into the fragility of this world. There was no point in arguing with him. I would only have reinforced his idea that I was a militant feminist, a convenient view to hide behind these days. I can only hope his wife never has to learn about the "other" problems.

As Eve says, "Money helps, but it doesn't keep you warm at night."

In addition, while on the outside you may come off as a super-strong feminist, really able to make it on your own, inside there are still the times when the old hurts come back.

Ellen comments, "It's hard to look at photographs because often there's such an image of joy: my husband and the kids, or me and the children, or me and my husband. This really breaks me up. I don't feel I can create that atmosphere for myself, by myself. I can't give the kids what I could give them when I had a husband."

Joyce's husband died three years ago, and she says, "For me, the year doesn't begin on January 1, but on April 24. When that date comes around, I say: 'My God, I've made it for another year. I've really survived.' "

Vera is somewhat bitter about her image and the role she has been forced to assume. "I firmly believe we are not underdogs seeking crumbs, but valiant women doing a job we didn't apply for. Above all, I don't feel I have survived yet. Not until my children are raised and out from under. My youngest is now two: that gives me nineteen more years to go."

A similarly strong viewpoint is held by Geraldine, who writes, "Nobody gives a damn. Widows have become the sacrificial victims of a mania for perennial immaturity, and dying has replaced sex as the great national taboo." Geraldine would like to see widows take a more militant stand to push through government programs, job training, image-raising, and more equitable financial plans which would assist all twelve million of us. In *Singles World* (May 1976), she stated, "I refuse to be a pacifist in this battle. I would like to see a national organization started that is devoted to the problems of widows. They must use

political power and influence to see that the organization
prospers, so that the stigma attached to the word 'widow'
will be replaced by recognition of accomplishments by
widows."

We are all proud of our accomplishments, of having
survived. But there remains that soft underbelly, the
memory of what was and what happened afterward that
can't be dismissed, no matter how many years have gone
by.

Aunt Rose had a bad headache after our interview and
told me later, "It really is painful to remember all the
past, as it hasn't been a pleasant one. I still cry when I
think how lonely it was for Anthony without a father, and
how I had to try so many different things to get ahead.
Well, we made it. I won't complain. I'll leave it all in
God's hands."

The memories are always there, and they are not
always wistful. Sometimes they can call forth amusing
times, and sometimes the memory of the man who was is
mixed up with the person you now are.

For Marilyn, "When I think of Paul now, I giggle or
smile, because I honestly can't remember anything sad or
unhappy about our marriage. But still, I'm not sure if he
were here now, whether we would marry or even love each
other, because I'm such a different person now than I was
ten years ago."

And Karen not only regrets that Bob couldn't see the
good developments in his children but that he wasn't
around to see and share the things that happened with
her. "I missed him so when David graduated, but when I
became a member of the school board, which he had run
for unsuccessfully some years before, I thought, here's one
for you, Bob—but God, how I wish he had really been
here to share it."

And of course, I feel that way, too, whenever I get a
book contract, or when I received the grant from Welles-

ley to research this book. Damn—the one person in the world who would really have appreciated it wasn't around to break open a bottle of champagne with.

And aside from the longing, the missing, there are still many times that are irritating and frustrating—but you do acquire a more jaded view about this. A few weeks ago I had to fill out still another government form. After sex identification, there were a series of boxes waiting to be checked off. They read: married, single, other. Well, I'm not married, but with three children I don't feel single, so I guess I'm an other. I thought that was funny, but I wouldn't have several months ago.

Some of the laughable things may seem like graveyard humor to "outsiders," but the widows I interviewed all had amusing anecdotes to tell. Somewhere along the line, you have to develop a sense of humor about your situation.

Intelligent, Not Bovine, Acceptance

You finally understand what has happened to you and where you're going. In his book, *America*, John Steinbeck wrote, "The result (of men working so hard, dying of stress, alcohol, etc.) is a great oversupply of widows, mostly reluctant or too old to remarry. In many cases they are able to live minimal lives on the insurance or investments which were part of the pressures which killed their husbands, for it is a bit of the American man's duty to live and act in the almost certain knowledge that his wife will survive him. And perhaps this very expectation has something to do with his demise . . . Many a hopeless widow is better endowed socially as well as sexually than the illiterate child-women, all hair and false bosoms, who so excite the American man."

Well, so be it. You will not be twenty again; you know you can't go "home" again. You want to go forward. Having gotten through the debacle, the recoil, or whatever any researcher wants to call it, having survived, you are a totally new and whole person—stronger, better, braver, and more understanding of "self" than you've ever been in your entire life.

You are no longer thinking of yourself as a widow, but as a person. And you are strong enough to admit that the growth process occurred because of your circumstances, that it was a tragic event that brought you to this new stage.

Dr. Phyllis Silverman, a widow herself and the Harvard sociologist who instituted Boston's successful widow-to-widow program, observed, "You never get over it. I think that you get used to it." Most of the widows I interviewed have a different feeling.

Tanya describes her widowhood as an "emotional odyssey." Further, "Taking the Karmic view, one does emerge a wholer and stronger person. Hard school of course, but I, too, feel that out of that awful time came numerous precious and valuable directions. So saith Pollyanna!"

Irene believes every woman should prepare herself for widowhood, even while married. "Learn about financial matters, know yourself as an individual within a marriage, not simply a dependent. I'm proud of my emotional stability and maturity now, worked on and earned from those hellish years."

Beth is also up on herself. "Finally I've arrived as my own person. I struggled with this constantly, even at the beginning, and it took me over four years to break free of my old identity."

Anne describes herself as "not religious, but I feel my husband is still with me, and I think he knows what is happening to me. Nothing is ever lost in the world; in a way he's still living, somehow."

Amy has much the same feeling. "When Wayne died, it was time for him to die. And I didn't really feel alone, and still don't. Somehow or other he is always a part of my life."

Eve feels strongly that "God has a reason for what he does. He apparently needed my first husband and later gave me another. I have no quarrel with God, and I try to do as he guides me."

Again, Nancy summed it up best. "Maybe that's the reason this experience came to you by fate. What a waste if you had never been able to realize yourself and what you are and what you can do! It would have been a waste if I had never come to the realization that I am a capable, independent, functioning person on my own, rather than just being somebody's wife."

APPENDIXES

Appendix One
Books on Grief, Widowhood

After The Flowers Have Gone, by Bea Decker and Gladys Kooiman (Zondervan Publishing House), 1973. An uplifting collection of anecdotes about Mrs. Decker's own experiences and other widows she tried to help.

Bereavement: Its Psychosocial Aspects, edited by Bernard Schoenberg, Irwin Gerber, Alfred Wiener, Austin H. Kutscher, David Peretz, and Arthur C. Carr (Columbia University Press), 1975. Case-histories of bereaved men and women and their confrontations with society.

The Book of Hope: How Women Can Overcome Depression, by Dr. Helen A. De Rosis and Victoria Y. Pellegrino (Macmillan), 1976. Eight out of every ten women suffer depression at some point in their lives. "It's an epidemic," say the authors. The book outlines components of depression, case histories, and most important, positive ways to deal with depression from group therapy to individual responses.

By Death or Divorce . . . It Hurts to Lose, by Amy Ross Young (Accent Books), 1976. The author has been through the traumatic experiences of both death and divorce. The book is sentimental, yet offers fresh ideas and guides to coping with this kind of grief.

Coping: A Survival Manual for Women Alone, by Martha Yates (Spectrum Books, Prentice-Hall), 1975. Down-to-earth suggestions for surviving in a couples-oriented society. For all single women.

Free to Be Good or Bad, by Herbert Holt, M.D. (M. Evans and Co.), 1976. An anti-improvement book that debunks a good many self-help approaches and provides reassurance and some effective self-help techniques.

Grief and How to Live With It, by Sarah Morris (Grosset & Dunlap), 1972. A gentle but firm approach for facing the pain and the demands placed on you by death.

Helping Each Other in Widowhood, by Phyllis Silverman, Ph.D. (Muler Press, New York), 1974. In addition to this book, reprints of other articles by Dr. Silverman are available by writing to her at Harvard University School of Medicine, Department of Community Psychiatry, Boston, Mass.

How to Survive the Loss of a Love, by Melba Colgrove, Ph.D., Harold H. Bloomfield, M.D., and Peter McWilliams (Lion Press, distributed by Simon & Schuster), 1976. A helpful and warm how-to book that covers many losses from that of a mate or money, to loss of youth, beauty, and sex drive or ability.

Lonely in America, by Suzanne Gordon (Simon & Schuster), 1976. Examines "singles" of all ages and backgrounds, and defines loneliness in its broadest ramifications, with its "feelings of hopelessness . . . which lead people to escape into relationships that . . . are only a means to an end rather than an end in themselves." The author herself says this "is not an upbeat book," but it is one which underlines the fact that you are not really alone and uncovers the ways people deal with their single state.

On Being Alone, Widowed Persons Service, Box 199, Long Beach, California 90801. A good overall guide to the problems of widowed men and women, well written by James A. Paterson and available free from this offshoot of the National Retired Teachers Association of Retired Persons and Action for Independent Maturity.

Religion and Bereavement, Health Services Publishing, 1972. A thoughtful collection of essays on grief, children, and other widows' problems by a group of clergymen of all denominations.

Survival Guide for the Suddenly Single, by Barbara Berson and Ben Bova (St. Martin's Press), 1974. Slanted more toward divorced readers, but interesting and amusing in the areas of social and sexual problems.

What Does She Do Now? (a guidebook for widows and those called upon to aid widows), LIMRA, 170 Sigourney Street, Hartford, Connecticut 06105. This free booklet takes the reader from the immediate problems of death (including making funeral arrangements) to the routines for receiving Social Security, V.A. and other benefits, and dealing with life insurance, and the estate.

Widowhood in an American City, by Helen Z. Lopata (Schenkman Publishing Co., Cambridge, Mass.), 1973. Case histories of the Widows Consultation Center in New York City.

Women Alone: A Practical Handbook for Widows and Divorcees, by Isabella Taves (Funk & Wagnall), 1968 (paperback). Interviews with widows and other single women on sex, finances, social and other problems.

Your Retirement Widowhood Guide, NRTA-AARP, P.O. Box 2400, Long Beach, California 90801. Aimed at older widows, this booklet takes you through the "seasons of grief" to practical advice about health and job-hunting. Available free.

Appendix Two
Widow-to-Widow Programs, Special Counseling

*NATIONWIDE PROGRAMS:

COPO
Catholic One Person Organization
Contact the Family Life Apostate Division of your local Catholic archdiocese for information.

NAIM Conference
109 N. Dearborn Street
Suite 901
Chicago, Illinois 60602
312-346-7876
NAIM helps widows and widowers "psychologically, financially, legally, and spiritually," and is open to Catholics and spouses of deceased Catholics. Monthly meetings, social activities, speakers.

209

Contact Father Corcoran, the director, for information on local branches.

Parents Without Partners
7901 Woodmont Avenue
Bethesda, Maryland 20014
301-654-8850

An international, nonprofit, nonsectarian group "devoted to welfare and interests of single parents and their children." The annual membership of $13.00 includes local and national newsletters. Activities include group discussions, social events, family outings. Your own reaction very much depends on the local group you join. Some widows have found P.W.P. marvelous; others have hated it. For information, contact Virginia Martin, Acting Director.

Post Cana Conference
1200 17th Street, N.W.
Room 306
Washington, D.C. 20036
202-659-6600

National headquarters for this Catholic action group.

Theos Foundation
11609 Frankstown Road
Pittsburgh, Pennsylvania 15235
412-243-4299

Bea Decker, the executive director, is also coauthor of *After The Flowers Have Gone.* THEOS stands for "They Help Each Other Spiritually" and is a nondenominational group for young and middle-aged widows and widowers. It conducts discussion groups, social activities, and person-to-person help. There are more than thirty chapters in Pennsylvania, Texas, California, Florida, Illinois, Ohio, Oregon and Canada. Contact the main office for local groups.

Widow-to-Widow Program
Action for Independent Maturity (AIM)
1909 K. Street, N.W.
Washington, D.C. 20049
202-872-4922

Directed by Leo E. Baldwin, this nationwide group trains widows for out-reach and hot-line programs in communities throughout the U.S.

Widowed Persons Service
National Office
1909 K. Street, N.W.
Washington, D.C. 20049
202-872-4700

This service is another program of the NRTA-AARP group with an aim of working on a one-to-one basis with recent widows or widowers. Widows are referred to the service by ministers, family friends; but for direct information, contact the national office, above, also under the direction of Leo E. Baldwin, who will provide addresses of local representatives.

LOCAL PROGRAMS: CALIFORNIA

The Widowed to Widowed Program
13133 Julian Avenue
Lakeside, California 92040
714-291-7900

The Widowed to Widowed Program
6655 Alvarado Road
San Diego, California 92120
714-291-7900

Director Helen Antoniak is clearly a hard-working, hard-pressed, sympathetic woman who has personally organized this successful widow-to-widow group. The slogan of her program is "We know what it is like. Let us help you." And she can help you if you live in the San Diego area. But if you want to live someplace else and need information and training materials to set up your own program, please send a self-addressed stamped envelope, and even a donation if you can afford one.

The Jewish Family Service of
San Francisco Peninsula and Marin County
1600 South Scott
San Francisco, California 94115
415-567-8860

CONNECTICUT

The Widows and Widowers Associates
Council of Churches of Greater Bridgeport
3030 Park Avenue
Bridgeport, Connecticut 06604
203-374-9471
   A social club with chapters throughout Connecticut.

Care-Giving
71 Bons Avenue
New Haven, Connecticut 06513
203-624-6744
   Under the direction of Peg Berg, this group runs a hot-line staffed by widowed volunteers.

GEORGIA

Widowed Persons Service for Atlanta Area
230 Peachtree Street, N.W.
Suite 2210
Atlanta, Georgia 30303
404-377-9901

MASSACHUSETTS

The Jewish Widow-Widowers Club
Beth El Temple Center
2 Concord Avenue
Belmont, Massachusetts 02178
617-484-6668
   Mrs. Eleanor Lubin is president of this "strictly local" organization with no branches or central organization. "We have monthly meetings and two special cocktail or dinner meetings with speakers and discussion groups." They are not a dating or matching club in any sense, even though they do have male members.

Widow to Widow Program
Harvard University Medical School
Department of Community Psychiatry
Boston, Massachusetts
617-743-3300

This program is under the direction of Dr. Phyllis Silverman, the widow and psychologist who first recognized the need for self-help programs spearheaded by widows who had "been there."

MICHIGAN

The Coordinating Council of
Widowed Services: Southeastern Michigan
c/o McComb County Community College
14500 Twelve Mile Road
Warren, Michigan 48093
   Establishes and coordinates self-help programs for widowed persons in and around greater Detroit area.

Widow to Widow Club
P.O. Box 08036
Detroit, Michigan 48208
313-863-7301
   Organized by the Stinson Funeral Home, the program is based on Dr. Silverman's experience and now has about 400 members, who were originally served by Stinson's—a rather unique extension of the Funeral Director's role.

MINNESOTA

Fellowship of the Concerned
Wesley Temple
Minneapolis, Minnesota 55400
612-339-0585

NEW JERSEY

AIM'S Widowed Persons Service
for Morris County
95 Mount Kemble Avenue
Morristown, New Jersey 07960
201-267-9720
   Mrs. Mildred Trotman is president of this outreach program, staffed by widowed volunteers. The group also runs a hot-line.

214 ALONE AND SURVIVING

COPO
(Catholic One Parent Organization)
Mrs. Mafalda Arrabito,
First Vice President
COPO
374 Marvin Avenue
Hackensack, New Jersey 07601

Three Northern New Jersey chapters:

Mr. John Burns, President
COPO
444 Mt. Prospect Avenue
Newark, New Jersey 07104

Mr. John Kovack, President
COPO
761 Thomas Street
Elizabeth, New Jersey 07202

Ecumenical Singles Congregation
of Bergen County
Cherry Hill Reformed Church
River Edge, New Jersey 07661
201-487-4828
Under the direction of Rev. Eltje Brunemeyer, this church group is the first of its kind in northern New Jersey, and is specifically orient- ed toward widowed and divorced people. In addition to services twice a month, the group plans social events, dinners, theater trips.

Somerset-Hunterdon WOWS
(Widows or Widowers)
Mr. Al Dytch, President
515 Immy Place
Bound Brook, New Jersey 08805
A nonsectarian, nonprofit group sponsored by the Family Life Bureau of the Diocese of Trenton. It provides rap sessions and social activities for 265 members, who pay $5.00 annual dues.

NEW YORK

Albany Jewish Family Services
291 State Street
Albany, New York 12210
518-462-4291

Widow and Widowers Program
Bronx Municipal Hospital
Pelham Parkway South
and Eastchester Road
Bronx, New York 10461
212-430-8452
Rosemary Cucuzzo, a registered nurse, directs these social and support groups for Bronx residents.

Grief Groups
262 Coleridge Street
Brooklyn, New York 11235
212-646-5537
Roberta Temes directs a private practice run by social workers and psychologists. Discussion groups are for adults and children. The fee is $10.00 per session (adjustable depending on income).

Family Service Society
181 Franklin Street
Buffalo, New York 14202
716-849-1515
Child and Family Services will refer you to Widows/Widowers group.

The Postgraduate Center for Mental Health
124 East 28th Street
New York, New York 10016
212-689-7700, ext. 740 or 842
A new program for widowed or divorced men and women. The goal is to develop solutions and a new lifestyle through the sharing of legal, financial, and emotional problems via group discussions. Lectures, films, study groups are planned.

Task Force on Jewish Singles
Federation of Jewish Philanthropies
130 East 59th Street
New York, New York 10022
212-751-1000
Brochures and newsletters on Jewish singles.

Family Service of Westchester
470 Mamaroneck Avenue
White Plains, New York 10605
914-948-8004

Linda Gilberto is the director of this active widow and widowers group with 400 members in New York's Westchester County. Members are involved in this "outreach" program in which the need to talk about one's grief is a primary concern. There are eight branches throughout Westchester—a model for other groups across the country.

OHIO

Widows and Widowers
108 Wyngate Drive
Dayton, Ohio 45429
513-293-9074

Contact director Mrs. Catherine Chakrian for information.

TEXAS

Widowed, Inc.
1111 Lovette Boulevard
Houston, Texas 77006
713-528-5511

VIRGINIA

Quatrefoil
8303 Oxbow Court
Alexandria, Virginia 22308
703-280-1004

Eugene Eveslage is president of this nonsectarian social club for widows under 45 and widowers under 50.

WASHINGTON

**Widows' Information and
Consultation Service**
1005 ½ S.W. 152nd Street
Seattle, Washington 98166
206-246-6142

This nonprofit group for widowed men and women has a staff of volunteers, under the direction of Wendy Morgan, who assist widows personally and offer information about community resources. The service also sponsors rap groups and social activities and publishes a monthly newsletter.

WISCONSIN

Widows or Widowers, Inc.
3201 West Highland Boulevard
Milwaukee, Wisconsin 53220
414-342-1633

Appendix Three
Organizations and Books for Counseling Children

Dare to Discipline, by James Dobson (Tyndale House), 1976. Specific, practical guidance on expressing love and authority; written by a psychologist.

Learning to Say Goodbye (When a Parent Dies), by Paul Giovanopoulos (Macmillan), 1976. The author has hosted the television show, "How Do Your Children Grow," and in this book discusses with children, parents, and professionals how to deal with grief. He covers the questions, fears, fantasies kids have when a parent dies and reports on the stages of mourning they must work through.

MOMMA, c/o Jean Townsend, 2030 E. 4th Street, Suite 240, Santa Ana, California 92705. An organization of ̄ingle mothers (divorced, widowed, unmarried) that holds rap groups on housing, child care, the importance of father figures, etc.

219

MOMMA: The Sourcebook for Single Mothers, edited by Karol Hope and Nancy Young (NAL/Plume), 1976. Compiled by members of MOMMA, a national organization of single mothers. Useful information on child care, welfare and legal rights to encourage the 7,000,000 mothers who are on their own.

The Myth of the Happy Child, by Carol Klein (Harper & Row), 1975. The author, who also wrote *The Single Parent Experience*, looks at the problems of anxiety, grief, and fear. *Publishers Weekly* said, "A valuable addition to the literature which may help adults understand and help children cope with their fears, anxieties, loneliness . . ."

P.E.T.: Parent Effectiveness Training, by Dr. Thomas Gordon (Meridian Books), 1975. How to listen to kids, how to feed back what we hear, how to express our own feelings in a way that helps the entire family. *P.E.T. in Action*, by Dr. Thomas Gordon (Wyden Books), 1976, includes interviews and case studies on hang-ups and emotions of parents and the problems and resistance of children from toddlers to teens.

The Single Parent Resource Center, 3896 24th Street, San Francisco, California 94114 (415) 821-7058. Director Carol Jauch, who is a single mother, says, "Ninety-five percent of single mothers are having trouble making ends meet, and emotionally they're saddled with guilt feelings about bringing up their children alone." Workshops at the center deal with specific problems; there are informal social gatherings, and a Childcare Switchboard helps locate suitable child care services. The center also publishes "The Single Parent Journal," available for $1.00.

Teaching Your Child to Cope With Crisis, by Suzanne Ramos (McKay), 1975. The author, a specialist in child-rearing, gives straight answers for adults who must deal with children's problems including death, moving, financial worries, etc.

Toddlers And Parents, by T. Berry Brazelton (Delacorte Press/Seymour Lawrence), 1974. A broad view of raising toddlers with special sections on the problems of single parents.

Appendix Four
Financial Guidance and Information

BANKS WITH WOMEN'S DIVISIONS:

Alabama: Fifteen banks owned by First Alabama Bancshares, Inc.
Illinois: La Salle National Bank; The First National Bank of Chicago.
New York: The Bank of New York (established a women's banking department over a century ago); The First Women's Bank of New York City.

Other women's banks are underway in San Francisco, Los Angeles, San Diego, Seattle, Chicago, Greenwich (Conn.), and Washington, D.C.

Brokerage Firms With Women's Departments: Oppenheimer & Co.; E. F. Hutton, which offers investment reviews, educational seminars, and a question-answering service; and Bache & Co., which runs seminars on investments for women.

Credit Discrimination Problems: For help, contact your local Human Rights Agencies, Civil Liberties or Women's Liberation Organizations, and consumer reporters of your local newspaper.

Financial Problems with Banks: Send complaints to the Banking Department or Commission of your state. For a federally chartered bank, contact The Office of the Comptroller of the Currency, Washington, D.C. 20219 or The Federal Home Loan Bank Board, 101 Indiana Avenue, N.W., Washington, D.C. 20522.

BOOKS, PAMPHLETS, BROCHURES ON FINANCES

Borrowing Basics for Women
First National City Bank
Public Affairs Department
P.O. Box 939
Church Street Station
New York, New York 10008

A comprehensive booklet, with an introduction by Bess Myerson, ranging from how to establish or re-establish credit to applying for loans and managing money, as well as a glossary of credit terms.

The Economics of Being a Woman (Or What Your Mother Never Told You), by Dee Dee Ahern and Betsy Bliss (Macmillan), 1976. Whether you're a widow, a total woman, or a feminist, this will provide good guidelines for economic competence and financial know-how. A whole gamut of dealing with dollars from credit lines to investments.

Federal Tax Guide for Survivors, Executors, and Administrators
Publication #559, 1977 Edition

Published by the Department of the Treasury, Internal Revenue Service. To obtain a copy, contact your nearest I.R.S. office.

The Financial Facts of Widowhood
(How to Prepare Your Wife to Be a Widow)
Anchor National Financial Services, Inc.
Phoenix, Arizona 85016
602-956-8750

The grim facts, with some more up-key directives about what to do about finances once you are widowed. Free from Anchor directly or local offices of this coast-to-coast financial counseling service.

Let's Talk About Money
Consumer and Community Services
American Council of Life Insurance
277 Park Avenue
New York, New York 10017
212-922-3000
A practical guide to insurance, investments, and money management. Free.

Social Security: The Fraud in Your Future, by Warren Shore (Macmillan), 1976. A newsman exposes all the inequities and inconsistencies of the Social Security system and provides answers to some of the most pressing problems pertinent to widows.

Women and Social Security: Adapting to a New Era
U.S. Government Printing Office
Washington, D.C. 20402
A recent paper prepared by the Task Force on Women and Social Security. (Enclose 50¢)

Appendix Five
Employment Counseling and Information

Business and Professional Women's Foundation
2012 Massachusetts Avenue
Washington, D.C. 20036
202-293-1100
   Administers several funding and scholarship programs to foster career advancement or training for women 30 and over.

Consumer Guide's New Job Opportunities for Women, by Muriel Lederer and the Editors of Consumer Guide (Simon & Schuster), 1976.

Information Center on the Mature Woman
515 Madison Avenue
New York, New York 10022
212-826-3300
   Provides bibliographies and directories on jobs, education possibilities, legal, and financial assistance.

The Institute for the Study of Women in Transition
5 Market Street
Portsmouth, New Hampshire 03810
603-436-0981

Explores alternatives for single women in the areas of occupations, finance, politics, health, sex. Last year this group sponsored a conference on "Older Women Alone." They will send announcements of upcoming events.

Job-Finding Techniques for Mature Women
Women's Bureau
Superintendent of Documents
U.S. Government Printing Office
Washington, D.C. 20402
(Enclose 30¢)

New Directions for Women
Box 27
Dover, New Jersey 07801

A quarterly detailing employment news and training opportunities. Subscription is $3.00 a year

Women's Information Service (WISE)
38 South Main Street
Hanover, New Hampshire 03755
603-643-5133

This service provides free counseling for finding a job or planning a new career.

Women's Resource Center
226 Bostwick, N.E.
Grand Rapids, Michigan 49603
616-456-8571

This center uses a $100,000 grant from the Ford Foundation to help mature West Michigan women find work, go back to school, or develop new skills. For information, contact Jan Blaich.

Appendix Six
Social Groups and Clubs: "Introduction" Services

We are listing representative groups in the New York metropolitan area. For sources in your city or state, check the local yellow pages under "Social Clubs," "Dating Services," "Introduction Services," and "Personal Service Organizations."

Central Registry Matching Service
P.O. Box 6881
Jersey City, New Jersey 07306
201-451-8719
   A New York/New Jersey offshoot of the Singles' Alumni Club, this computerized match-up service has an extensive application and a membership fee of $77.00 per year, with a guarantee of ten dates and a "maximum of unlimited matches."

Dinner Parties Unlimited
Department V
501 Fifth Avenue
New York, New York 10017
212-661-4665

Dinner and theater parties, sports, socials, lectures, discussions, walking tours, bus trips—all for single people. "Best of all, good company and intelligent conversation." Membership is eighteen dollars per year.

Insight Dynamics
New York Office:
369 Lexington Avenue
New York, New York 10017
212-682-2040
Toll free: 800-421-8500
Los Angeles: 213-654-4000

Twelve-hour seminars to "release your potential for love, success, health, happiness, and prosperity." Tuition is sixty-five dollars for seminar. Other fees depend on how far you want to extend your singles connection—social events, lectures.

The Party Vine
Mr. Doug Russell, President
204 East 77th Street
New York, New York 10017
212-861-4144

For "college graduates" who want to meet people of the same caliber. Publishes monthly newsletter of singles events in New York City and suburbs. Also holds twice-monthly cheese and wine-tasting parties. Yearly membership is $18.00.

Video-Date

New Jersey:	**Washington:**
1810 Springfield Avenue	1656 33rd Street, N.W.
Maplewood, New Jersey 07040	Washington, D.C. 20007
201-761-5069	202-333-6460

Video-taped dating service, no contracts, free demonstration, free brochures. Three month membership is $125.00. Directed by Stan Subarsky.

Video-Mate
216 East 49th Street
New York, New York 10017
212-371-2130

Video-tapes are the vehicle for matching up single men and women of compatible ages, background, interests, and education. Six hundred clients pay $125.00 for a three-month contract and may renew every three months afterward for half the original fee.

View A Date
10342 Old Olive Street Road
St. Louis, Missouri 63141
314-432-2330

Connie Majkut directs this videotaped dating service. The fee is $50.00 for three month membership.

Widows Travel Club
Tausig Travel, Inc.
17 East 45th Street
New York, New York 10017
212-697-4000

Mrs. Beatrice L. Green, the club's director, started her travel matchmaking services as a favor for a friend. Now she has members from every state and has paired up hundreds of widows of compatible background, interests, and age who don't want to travel alone. The annual membership fee of $15.00 required, as well as answering a questionnaire and providing a photograph of yourself.

Index

231